Library Resources for Singers, Coaches, and Accompanists

Library Resources for Singers, Coaches, and Accompanists

An Annotated Bibliography, 1970–1997

Compiled by Ruthann Boles McTyre

Music Reference Collection, Number 71

Greenwood Press
Westport, Connecticut • London

Library of Congress Cataloging-in-Publication Data

McTyre, Ruthann Boles, 1954–
    Library resources for singers, coaches, and accompanists : an
annotated bibliography, 1970–1997 / Ruthann Boles McTyre.
        p.   cm.—(Music reference collection, ISSN 0736-7740 ; no.
71)
    Discographies and videographies: p.
    Includes indexes.
    ISBN 0–313–30266–9 (alk. paper)
    1. Singing—Instruction and study—Sources—Bibliography.
I. Title.   II. Series.
ML128.V7M4   1998
016.783—dc21   98–23959
                              MN

British Library Cataloguing in Publication Data is available.

Library of Congress Catalog Card Number: 98–23959
ISBN: 0–313–30266–9
ISSN: 0736-7740

First published in 1998

Greenwood Press, 88 Post Road West, Westport, CT 06881
An imprint of Greenwood Publishing Group, Inc.

Printed in the United States of America

The paper used in this book complies with the
Permanent Paper Standard issued by the National
Information Standards Organization (Z39.48–1984).

10 9 8 7 6 5 4 3 2

Dedicated to my husband George.

Contents

Preface

The purpose of this bibliography is to provide a doorway into the vast world of library resources for anyone who deals with study of voice, whether a voice teacher, student, performer, vocal coach, or accompanist. It is intended to be a practical guide to library materials that aid and enhance the study of voice. Readers should note that choral music is not treated in this volume, but rather materials that deal with repertoire, bibliographic guides, plot synopses, translations, guides to diction, pedagogy, stage resources, and so on, that are related to opera, musical theater and the solo voice. The period covered is 1970 to 1997.

In the preliminary stages of research, it was quickly discovered that certain limitations had to be established in order to complete the bibliography in a timely fashion. First of all, 1970 was chosen as the starting date for inclusion. Admittedly, this caused omission of a great many significant titles from the bibliography; however, many of them do not escape mention. Hopefully by going to the library shelves to locate the titles included, readers will take it upon themselves to look to the right and left of the chosen title and see what other books fall in the same category. It is for this reason that I refer to the bibliography as a "doorway." It will lead singers and teachers to the many other resources available to them in their library.

Secondly, it was decided that books titled "The Operas of...." and "The Songs of..." would be omitted. One has only to try a title search in OCLC to understand why. It was also decided that only English language sources would be included.

Last of all, the maximum number of entries for each section has been set at forty. Having recently finished work as a contributing writer for the fifth edition of *Music Reference and Research Materials* (Duckles/Reed, Schirmer,

1997), with a limit of fifty titles for my assigned section, it seemed that forty titles was a reasonable number for the current volume. In some instances, a section will fall short of that number; in others, difficult choices were made. Any errors or omissions are entirely my own and I welcome any comments or criticisms.

This bibliography is also intended for use in reference departments in libraries. It is my hope that those who work in reference departments will pull out their pencils and jot call numbers in the margins for ready reference. Given the popularity of song literature questions in all types of libraries, both public and academic, this volume will hopefully prove to be a frequently-consulted resource itself, leading both the librarian and the patron to the source that will answer such questions.

The book is divided into ten chapters, each focusing on a particular type of library resource that pertains to the study of voice in some fashion. Included in these prefatory pages is a bibliographic essay on general music reference sources, graciously compiled and written by Ida Reed, music librarian and most recent editor of *Music Reference and Research Materials: An Annotated Bibliography*. Ms. Reed was the person who said to me, "I have an idea for a book that I think you should investigate." And here it is. My thanks to Ida for suggesting it to me. She has been my teacher and dear friend for many years, and the idea for this bibliography is only one thing for which I owe her gratitude.

Thanks, too, to Sarah E. McCleskey, who has served as my indexer, proofreader, and cheerleader, all in the midst of finishing her degree in library science and writing her graduate paper. Ms. Pat Bibb, Administrative Assistant for Social Science and Humanities Reference in the Baylor Libraries deserves a great deal of thanks for her work in formatting the manuscript.

My thanks is also extended to Dr. Avery T. Sharp, Dean of Libraries at Baylor University, for allowing me a summer's leave to work on the manuscript and to my colleagues both on the library faculty and in the School of Music for their support and encouragement. Professor Jack Coldiron deserves extra thanks for time spent and knowledge and resources shared. To my wonderful staff at the Crouch Music and Fine Arts Library-John Amagliani, Patty Bellus, David Faulkner, James Floyd, Mary Goolsby, Sha Towers, and Lesley Wilson-I offer my gratitude and thanks for absolutely everything.

Finally, thanks to my husband George, who has been a constant source of support throughout this project and who has had the wisdom when to ask about its progress and more importantly, when not to do so.

General Music Reference

BIBLIOGRAPHIES

0.1   Duckles, Vincent H., and Ida Reed. *Music Reference and Research Materials.* 5th edition. xvii + 812 pp. New York: Schirmer Books, 1997.

0.2   Brockman, William. *Music: A Guide to the Reference Literature.* xv + 254 pp. Littleton, Colo.: Libraries Unlimited, Inc., 1987.

0.3   Crabtree, Phillip D., and Donald H. Foster. *Sourcebook for Research in Music.* xii + 236 pp. Bloomington: Indiana University Press, 1993.

0.4   Balay, Robert. *Guide to Reference Books.* 11th edition. 2,020 pp. Chicago: American Library Association, 1996.

0.5   Jackson, Roland. *Performance Practice, Medieval to Contemporary: A Bibliographic Guide.* xxix + 518 pp. New York: Garland Publishing, 1988.

0.6   Schuursma, Ann Briegleb. *Ethnomusicology Research: A Select Annotated Bibliography.* xxvii + 173 pp. New York: Garland Publishing, 1992.

0.7   Phelps, Roger P., Lawrence Ferrara, and Thomas W. Goolsby. *A Guide to Research in Music Education.* 4th ed. 367 pp. Metuchen, N.J.: The Scarecrow Press, 1993.

Thousands of titles that can be called "music reference works" exist. Finding the help needed to answer a particular question about music, be it completing the information necessary for a recital program or understanding the variety of interpretations of a work, can often be done more easily with a basic knowledge of these reference works. A number of books are available to guide their users through the forest of titles. The oldest and largest of these is *Music*

Reference and Research Materials, whose 5th edition is by Vincent H. Duckles and Ida Reed; now listing and describing over 3,800 books, this work can be a good beginning to finding needed information. Its listings are arranged by subject covered and there is a detailed index which gives additional guidance. If the information provided about a book can occasionally seem too brief, often information on reviews of the work is provided. If yet still more information is needed, 558 of the titles are given more thorough description by William Brockman in *Music: A Guide to the Reference Literature.* Since the descriptions of music reference works these two books provide can be so helpful, numbers listing locations in these two works will be given for the rest of the works discussed in this essay, with the prefix "D" indicating a location in Duckles-Reed (although edition may occasionally differ) and "B" indicating the work's place in Brockman. (The location number for Duckles/Reed and Brockman are D4.22, B5 and D4.12, respectively.) There is yet a third title of this type, *Sourcebook for Research in Music* (D4.18), by Phillip D. Crabtree and Donald H. Foster, containing little description but a wider list of titles, also arranged by subjects covered. The information provided in these three works should go a long way toward answering a user's general music questions and helping to locate reference books in specific areas of music.

There also exists a number of general reference works which are organized much like Duckles and which give a wide subject view of the variety of books to be found in a large general reference library. Under the sponsorship of the American Library Association (ALA), the *Guide to Reference Books* (D4.41) from the early part of the century has been written and edited by working librarians who use many of these reference books in their daily research. Now in its eleventh edition, edited by Robert Balay and written by a scholarly corps of reference specialists, the *Guide* is a bibliography covering the most useful general reference works, as well as works in the humanities (including music), the social and behavioral sciences, history and area studies, and science, technology, and medicine. While no single work can be comprehensive, this title certainly comes close. The detailed index of authors and titles can help the user find specific works. There are also many specialized music bibliographies that are of great assistance to the beginning researcher, each covering a specific area of music. Two of these, Roland Jackson's *Performance Practice, Medieval to Contemporary: A Bibliographic Guide* (D3.74), and Ann Briegleb Schuursma's *Ethnomusicology Research: A Select Annotated Bibliography* (D4.189), cover two subject areas given renewed and increased attention in the last decade or so. Another area is covered in *A Guide to Research in Music Education* (D4.285), whose fourth edition, by Roger P. Phelps, Lawrence Ferrara, and Thomas W. Goolsby contains a solid bibliographical section of major work in the field (pp. 333-358).

GENERAL MUSIC ENCYCLOPEDIAS AND DICTIONARIES
THE NEW GROVE FAMILY

0.8   Sadie, Stanley. *The New Grove Dictionary of Music and Musicians.*
        20 vols. London: Macmillan; Washington, D. C.: Grove's
        Dictionaries of Music, 1980.

0.9   Sadie, Stanley. *The New Grove Dictionary of Musical Instruments.* 4
        vols. London: Macmillan; Washington, D. C.: Grove's Dictionaries
        of Music, 1984.

0.10   Hitchcock, H. Wiley, and Stanley Sadie. *The New Grove Dictionary of
        American Music.* 4 vols. London: Macmillan; Washington, D. C.:
        Grove's Dictionaries of Music, 1986.

0.11   Krummel, Donald W., and Stanley Sadie. *Music Printing and
        Publishing.* xiv + 615 pp. New York: W.W. Norton, 1990.

0.12   Sadie, Stanley, and Christina Bashford. *The New Grove Dictionary of
        Opera.* 4 vols. London: Macmillan; Washington, D. C.: Grove's
        Dictionaries of Music, 1992.

The title generally regarded as the major music reference work in
English is *The New Grove Dictionary of Music and Musicians* (D1.48, B20),
edited by Stanley Sadie, the sixth edition of a work written by almost 2,500
contributors. Subjects covered include the areas of music history, theory and
practice, music terminology, various national musics (in geographic areas
ranging in size from a whole continent down to a city), and a large number of
biographies (stressing composers, but also including perfomers and people in the
business of music, such as printers, instrument makers, impresarios, and
performers). The entries for the composers who are judged to be among the
more important of those cited include a works list and a bibliography (whose
entries are in the European style, identifying the author by first initial and last
name, and omitting the publisher's name-this form should not be regarded as a
model to be used in most American situations); many of these articles on
individual composers have been published in logical groupings in less expensive
editions, easily identified by titles beginning "The New Grove." While there is
no index to this work, there are entries in Duckles which describe some of the
more useful articles to the music researcher: "Analysis," (D3.3), "Bibliography
of Music" (D13.11), "Dictionaries and Encyclopedias of Music" (D1.1),
"Editions, Historical" (D5.504), "Libraries," (D7.2), "Musicology," (D3.15),
"Periodicals" (D4.66), and various articles on "Sources" (D5.523, D5.530,
D5.542, D 5.583). Other prominent reference works evolved from The New
Grove: *The New Grove Dictionary of Musical Instruments* (B66, D1.488),
edited by Stanley Sadie; *The New Grove Dictionary of American Music* (B65,
D1.220), edited by H. Wiley Hitchcock and Stanley Sadie; *Music Printing and*

Publishing (D9.1), by D.W. Krummel and Stanley Sadie, *The New Grove Dictionary of Opera* (D1.469), edited by Stanley Sadie and Christina Bashford.

BIOGRAPHICAL SOURCES

0.13   Slonimsky, Nicolas. *Baker's Biographical Dictionary of Musicians.* 8th ed. xxxv + 2,115 pp. New York: Schirmer Books, 1991.

0.14   Slonimsky, Nicolas. *The Concise Edition of Baker's Biographical Dictionary of Musicians.* vi + 1,155 pp. New York: Schirmer Books, 1994.

0.15   Kostelanetz, Richard. *The Portable Baker's Biographical Dictionary of Musicians.* 291 pp. New York: Schirmer Books, 1995.

0.16   Slonimsky, Nicolas. *Baker's Biographical Dictionary of Twentieth-Century Classical Musicians.* 1,595 pp. New York: Schirmer Books, 1997.

0.17   Randel, Don Michael. *The Harvard Biographical Dictionary of Music* 1,013 pp. Cambridge, Mass. and London, England: The Belknap Press of Harvard University Press, 1996.

0.18   Bull, Storm. *Index to Biographies of Contemporary Composers.* 3 vols. Metuchen, N.J.: The Scarecrow Press, 1964-87.

0.19   Greene, Frank. *Composers on Record: An Index to Biographical Information on 14,000 Composers in 200 Reference Books.* xxxi + 604 pp. Metuchen, N.J.: The Scarecrow Press, 1985.

0.20   Hixon, Donald L., and Don A. Hennessee. *Women in Music: An Encyclopedic Biobibliography.* 2nd ed. 2 vols. Metuchen, N. J.: The Scarecrow Press, 1994.

0.21   Cummings, David. M. *International Who's Who in Music and Musicians' Directory (in the Classical and Light Classical Fields).* 14th ed. 1,296 pp. Cambridge, England: International Who's Who in Music, 1994.

While *The New Grove* does contain much bibliographic information, there also are many dictionaries containing only biographies; the foremost of these, originally by Theodore Baker, is *Baker's Biographical Dictionary of Musicians* (B80, D1.62), whose eighth (and latest) edition was compiled by Nicolas Slonimsky. Just as has happened with *The New Grove*, Baker's has expanded into a number of variant editions: *The Concise Edition of Baker's Biographical Dictionary of Musicians*, *The Portable Baker's Biographical Dictionary of Musicians* edited by Richard Kostelanetz, and *Baker's Biographical Dictionary of Twentieth-Century Classical Musicians* are all based on the 8th edition of Baker's, and other derivative works are expected to appear in the next few years. The entries in Baker's are not as thorough and the bibliographies are considerably shorter, but there are more than can be found in any other single volume dictionary. They begin with a brief description of the subject, the subject's specialty, and, usually, an adjective evaluating the subject's worth in the editor's opinion; for example: "Callas, Maria, celebrated soprano." The preface carefully explains the research necessary to have produced an accurate and well-written work of this type and the individual entries, on occasion, make clear to the careful reader the editor's famous sense of humor.

Baker's is a biographical dictionary which contains information on many classical musicians and some of the most familiar ones in the world of popular music. Another single-volume biographical dictionary, The Harvard Biographical Dictionary of Music has been compiled by Don Michael Randel, with the assistance of several contributing authors. It centers on the composers and performers of Western art and concert music, including jazz and popular music. There are also many other biographical dictionaries, some listed in the first chapter of Duckles, which limit themselves by subject; the coverage may include musicians of a particular region or nationality, musicians specializing in a particular kind of music (sacred, rock, or jazz, for instance) or musical occupation (musical instrument makers). The number of these dictionaries has made some indexers compile an assortment of helpful indexes to prevent the researcher from having to check many individual works when looking for elusive information. For example, Storm Bull compiled three volumes giving access to 275 works including information on composers, namely the Index to Biographies of Contemporary Composers (B376, D1.246); while the index itself, apart from location information, contains only the birth date and nationality of the composer, taking advantage of the organization Bull provides in these volumes can be a great time-saver. A similar source by Frank Greene, Composers on Record: An Index to Biographical Information on 14,000 Composers in 200 Reference Books (B388, D1.255) concentrates on composers with recorded works and helps by giving access to information on record jacket or in compact disc brochures, often more recent than can be found in book format. A recent thorough index to information on women musicians was compiled by Donald L. Hixon and Don A. Hennessee as Women in Music: An Encyclopedic Biobibliography (D1.257); this index, covering a multitude of musical specializations, includes a listing of those covered who work within each individual area.

Before leaving the subject of biographical dictionaries, one final title should be noted: the International Who's Who in Music and Musicians' Directory (B103, D1.70), published through the years by a number of different publishers in Cambridge, England, is a work that has appeared quite frequently in new editions. Its latest (14th) edition is the first in two volumes, with the first labelled as containing musicians (and others in the field of music) in "Classical and Light Classical" music and the second with "popular" musicians. Many of the entries were submitted, upon request, by the subjects themselves and contain not only the type of career information found in Baker's, but also listings of the subjects' hobbies and interests, with an address at which the subject can be reached.

MUSICAL TERMINOLOGY

0.22   Ammer, Christine. *The HarperCollins Dictionary of Music.* 512 pp. New York: HarperPerennial, 1995.

0.23   Randel, Don Michael. *The New Harvard Dictionary of Music.* xxi + 942 pp. Cambridge, Mass.: Belknap Press of Harvard University Press, 1986.

Concise definitions of a wide range of musical terminology in both popular and art music can be found in the 3rd edition of Christine Ammer's *The HarperCollins Dictionary of Music* (D1.5, B15). Included as well are helpful lists of various categories of music, musical examples and concise line drawings, as well as pronunciation guidance for many of the terms. *The New Harvard Dictionary of Music* (B36, D1.320), compiled by Don Michael Randel who was assisted by other experts in the field, contains longer definitions on fewer terms, and adds helpful though selective bibliographies to its format.

POPULAR MUSIC SOURCES:
THE GUINNESS FAMILY

0.24   Larkin, Colin. *The Guinness Encyclopedia of Popular Music.* 2nd ed., 6 vols. Enfield, Middlesex, England; New York: Guinness Publishers, Stockton Press, 1995.

0.25   *The Guinness Who's Who of Blues* . 2nd ed., 414 pp. 1995.

0.26   *The Guinness Who's Who of Country Music.* 473 pp. 1993.

0.27   *The Guinness Who's Who of Fifties Music.* 351 pp. 1993.

0.28   *The Guinness Who's Who of Film Musicals and Musical Films.* 351 pp. 1994.

0.29   *The Guinness Who's Who of Folk Music.* 320 pp. 1993.

0.30   *The Guinness Who's Who of Heavy Metal.* 2nd ed., 416 pp. 1995.

0.31   *The Guinness Who's Who of Indie and New Wave Music.* 2nd ed., 416 pp. 1995.

0.32   *The Guinness Who's Who of Jazz.* 508 pp. 1995.

0.33   *The Guinness Who's Who of Rap, Dance & Techno.* 348 pp. 1994.

0.34   *The Guinness Who's Who of Reggae.* 318 pp. 1994.
0.35   *The Guinness Who's Who of Seventies Music.* 457 pp. 1993.
0.36   *The Guinness Who's Who of Sixties Music.* 349 pp. 1992.
0.37   *The Guinness Who's Who of Soul Music.* 315pp. 1993.
0.38   *The Guinness Who's Who of Stage Musicals.* 382 pp. 1994.

While there are numerous single-volume reference works covering aspects of popular music, the most up-to-date and far-ranging series is, in the New Grove mode, based on *The Guinness Encyclopedia of Popular Music* (D1.397). The *Encyclopedia,* edited by Colin Larkin and a large team of experts in the various special areas, contains over 15,000 entries, most of which have lists of related recordings and videos as well as selected readings; the entries include information on performers, bands, writers, record labels, Broadway shows and pop music magazines from around the world, instruments, and manufacturers. Bold-face type is used within the articles to send the researcher to other relevant articles. There is also a general bibliography over 100 pages long. In addition, such separately issued paperbacks as listed above keep current the information covered in the larger work.

INTERNATIONAL INDEXES TO RESOURCES

0.39   *Répertoire International des Sources Musicales. (RISM)* 1960 - .
0.40   *Répertoire International de la Presse Musicale: A Retrospective Index Series (RIPM).* H. Robert Cohen, general editor. Ann Arbor, Mich.: UMI Center for Studies in Nineteenth-Century Music, University of Maryland, 1988- .
0.41   *The Music Index; A Subject-Author Guide to Current Music Periodical Literature.* Detroit, Mich.: Information Service, Inc., January 1949- . Vol. 1, no. 1- .
0.42   Répertoire International de Littérature Musicale. *RILM Abstracts of Music.* New York: International RILM Center, 1967- . Vol. 1- .

Three important music reference series are produced through the international cooperation of music libraries and scholars, making possible a wider scope than if done by a single nationality. *Répertoire International des Sources Musicales [RISM],* (D5.590) was begun in 1960 and has now a number of multi-volume series covering various types of music and theoretical writings on music (see also B423-432 and D4.376, 4.381, 4.383, 4.385, 4.386, 5.516, 5.520, 5.526, 5.546, 5.565, 5.571, 5.572, 5.582, 5.589, 5.599, 5.608, 5.622, and 7.1 for descriptions of the individual series); both early print editions and manuscript copies of music and music-connected titles can be found in this ongoing and enormous undertaking. Works in this series can be used to locate libraries holding original editions of Baroque or Classical era operas, oratorios or song collections, or for that matter, almost any music printed before 1801. In Series C of *RISM* (B174, D7.1), organized by country, can be found information on the libraries involved and their locations, histories, hours of opening, and their individual regulations for use. *Répertoire International de la Presse Musicale: A Retrospective Index Series (RIPM)* (D4.123), first published in 1988, is a series providing access to major 18th, 19th and early 20th century periodical literature dealing with music by indexing music periodicals and, occasionally, reprinting on microfilm the titles so indexed; for an index to periodical titles from 1949, see *Music Index* (B324; D4.889 and 12.11), which is available in both print and CD-ROM editions (See also 9.29). *Répertoire International de Littérature Musicale's RILM Abstracts of Music* (B327, D4.90), called *RILM* for short and begun in 1967, is an international quarterly journal of abstracts in English of current scholarly literature on music in all languages including books, articles, commentaries, prefaces to editions, dissertations, and reviews. *RILM* is also available on *OCLC's FirstSearch* and in CD-ROM format under the title *MUSE*.

CATALOGS

0.43   *OCLC*. 1971- . Online Computer Library Center, Inc.

0.44   *Research Librarians Information Network (RLIN)*.

0.45   *Dictionary Catalog of the Music Collection, New York Public Library.* 2nd ed. 44 vols. Boston, Mass.: G. K. Hall, 1982.

0.46   *Dictionary Catalog of the Music Collection of the Boston Public Library.* 20 vols. Boston, Mass.: G. K. Hall, 1972. *First Supplement.* 4 vols. Boston, Mass.: G. K. Hall, 1977.

0.47   *National Union Catalog: Pre-1956 Imprints: A Cumulative Author List Representing Library of Congress Printed Cards and Titles Reported by Other American Libraries.* 685 vols. London: Mansell, 1968-1981. *Supplement.* 68 vols. 1980-81.

To have an overview of the music cataloged and available for use in many American and a few foreign libraries, two large and ever-increasing databases are available: The online catalogs of the *Online Computer Library Catalog (OCLC)* (D12.1) and the *Research Libraries Information Network (RLIN*, pronounced "Ar-lin") (D12.2) list in an electronically accessible fashion the music material available from their individual member libraries and give bibliographic information for each title. These two services thus make available to the user a vast array of books on music, scores, and sound recording (in a variety of formats) and are a most valuable help when trying to identify a specific work or for an even more specific edition of that work. Before these services were available, library users had to rely on book catalogs of individual library holdings. A number of these are still quite useful, as the older works will take a while to be entered online. Two of the major book catalogs of music collections are those for the music reference collections of the New York Public Library (B188; D7.362) and the Boston Public Library (B184; D7.82). The New York catalog was first published in 1965 in 33 volumes with Supplements in 1973 and 1976 that were cumulated in second edition, published in 1982, 44 volumes; the Boston work was published in 1972 in 20 volumes, with a four-volume Supplement (1977). Perhaps the most important dictionary catalog for general library users is the *National Union Catalog* (D5.23), which, in a printed format beginning in 1953 and ending in 1989, had a separately printed section for music and related materials and was cumulated every five years (B316-317; D5.21 and 5.22).

SOURCES FOR REPERTOIRE

0.48 *Music in Print Series.* Philadelphia, Pa.: Musicdata, 1974- .
0.49 Music Library Association. *A Basic Music Library: Essential Scores and Sound Recordings.* 3rd ed. 665 pp. Chicago: American Library Association, 1997.

If information on currently available music is wanted, the place to look for many categories of music is the *Music in Print* series (B483; D5.7), which covers sacred and secular choral music (D5.204 and 5.202), guitar music (D5.282), organ music (D5.232), classical vocal music (D5.340), orchestra music (D5.269), and string music (D5.293). The orchestra music series includes voice with orchestral accompaniment. And if the user wants to limit the music found to the basic repertoire, a good source that lists current available editions is the 3rd edition of *A Basic Music Library: Essential Scores and Sound Recordings*, compiled by the Music Library Association with Elizabeth Davis, coordinating editor. Its introduction states that it "represents the world in a way that is balanced and diverse, culturally and geographically."

AMERICAN RESOURCES

0.50 Krummel, Donald. W., Jean Geil, Doris J. Dyen, and Deane L. Root. *Resources of American Music History: A Directory of Source Materials from Colonial Times to World War II.*   463 pp.   Urbana, Ill.: University of Illinois Press, 1981.

OCLC and RLIN generally describe manuscripts as collections and in a quite basic manner. Collections of American research material related to music (printed and manuscript music, personal papers, and other archival material) produced up to the beginning of World War II can be found listed and described in *Resources of American Music History: A Directory of Source Materials from Colonial Times to World War II* (B 165; D 4.355). This was a project of the American Bicentennial, compiled with the help of many local correspondents who knew the musical background of their home territory quite well and thus were able to include descriptions of a number of important collections in this nationally accessible catalog for the first time.

WRITING RESOURCES

0.51   Wingell, Richard J. *Writing about Music: An Introductory Guide.* 2nd ed.. 160 pp. Upper Saddle River, N. J.: Prentice Hall, 1997.

0.52   Caldwell, John. *Editing Early Music.* 2nd ed. 135 pp.   Oxford: Clarendon Press; New York: Oxford Univeristy Press, 1995.

0.53   Basart, Ann P.   *Writing about Music: A Guide to Publishing Opportunities for Authors and Reviewers.* xxiv + 588 pp. Berkeley, Calif.: Fallen Leaf Press, 1989.

0.54   Fidler, Linda M., and Richard S. James. *International Music Journals.* 544 pp. New York: Greenwood Press, 1990.

0.55   Meggett, Joan M.   *Music Periodical Literature: An Annotated Bibliography.* 116 pp. Metuchen, N. J.: The Scarecrow Press, 1978.

0.56   Grout, Donald Jay and Claude V. Palisca.   *A History of Western Music.* 5th ed. 862 pp. New York: W.W. Norton, 1996.

0.57   Burbank, Richard. *Twentieth-Century Music.* xxi + 485 pp. New York: Facts on File, 1984.

0.58   Slonimsky, Nicolas. *Music Since* 1900. 5th ed. 1,260 pp. New York: Schirmer Books; Toronto: Maxwell Macmillan Canada, 1994.

0.59   Diamond, Harold J. *Music Analyses: An Annotated Guide to the Literature* . 716 pp. New York: Schirmer Books, 1991.

All types of assistance for writing papers on music are available. Richard J. Wingell's *Writing about Music: An Introductory Guide* (D3.62) gives information on writing and research methods, including bibliographic formats preferred by many authorities. John Caldwell's *Editing Early Music* (D3.46) takes a practical approach to the editing of early music into a standard modern edition. And, if the finished paper seems publishable, Ann P. Basart's *Writing about Music: A Guide to Publishing Opportunities for Authors and Reviewers* (D4.67) not only discusses likely periodicals to try but also has compiled a source that gives a contemporary picture of many standard music periodicals and their editorial policies. *International Music Journals* (D4.73), edited by Linda M. Fidler and Richard S. James, both evaluates and gives a short history of 181 major music journals stressing scholarship, performance, composition, discography and librarianship. Valuable and varied information on music periodicals and their indexing has been compiled by Joan M. Meggett in *Music Periodical Literature: An Annotated Bibliography* (B405; D4.114).

A good overview of Western art music can be found in *A History of Western Music* (B120; D2.15), by Donald Jay Grout and Claude V. Palisca. There is also a companion compact disc, *Concise Norton Recorded Anthology of Western Music*, usually cataloged separately in libraries, which supplies beginning sound recording access to the vast amount of music described in Grout/Palisca. The musical events of the last 100 years are more closely examined by Richard Burbank in *Twentieth-Century Music* and by the 5th edition of Nicolas Slonimsky's monumental *Music since 1900* (D2.84). Commentary on many of the major works of Western art music can be easily found using Harold J. Diamond's *Music Analyses: An Annotated Guide to the Literature* (B335; D4.133), which gives easy access to information contained in hundreds of English-language books on music.

LOCATING EDITIONS

0.60 Brook, Barry S., and Richard Viano. *Thematic Catalogues in Music: An Annotated Bibliography.* 2nd ed. 1 + 602 pp. Stuyvesant, N. Y.: Pendragon Press, 1997.

0.61 Köchel, Ludwig, Ritter van. *Chronologisch-thematisches Verzeichnis sämtlicher Tonwerke Wolfgang Amadeus Mozarts, nebst Angabe der verlorengegangen, angefangenen, von fremder Hand bearbeiten, zweifelhaften und unterschobenen Kompositionen.* 6th ed., edited by Franz Gieglin, Alexander Weinmann and Gerd Sievers. cxliii + 1,024 pp. Wiesbaden: Breitkopf & Härtel, 1964.

0.62 Schmieder, Wolfgang. *Thematisch-systematisches Verzeichnis der musikalischen Werke von Johann Sebastian Bach: Bach-Werke-Verzeichnis (BWV).* 2nd, revised and enlarged ed. xlvi + 1,014 pp. Wiesbaden: Breitkopf & Härtel, 1990.

0.63 Hill, George R. and Norris L. Stephens. *Collected Editions, Historical Series & Sets, & Monuments of Music: A Bibliography.* xliv + 1,349 pp. Berkeley, Calif.: Fallen Leaf Press, 1997.

0.64   Heyer, Anna Harriet.   *Historical Sets, Collected Editions, and Monuments of Music: A Guide to Their Contents*. 3rd ed. 2 vols. Chicago, Ill.: American Library Association, 1980.

Most of the sources discussed up to now have concerned writings on musical literature. There are also general music sources that help identify music works and available editions of them. The *New Grove Dictionary* has an article by Barry Brook on thematic catalogs of music and their history. In addition, Brook and Richard Viano have compiled *Thematic Catalogues in Music: An Annotated Bibliography* (B398; D4.13) which lists both print and manuscript catalogs; the introductory material hold much valuable information on the thematic catalog and its development.   Two particularly important thematic catalogs that even beginning musicians know of (although they may not realize it) are by Wolfgang Schmieder and Ludwig Köchel. Köchel organized one of the first thematic catalogs for the works of Wolfgang Amadeus Mozart in 1862, seventy-one years after the composer's death: *Chronologisch-thematisches Verzeichnis sämtlicher Tonwerke Wolfgang Amadeus Mozarts, nebst Angabe der verlorengegangen, angefangenen, von fremder Hand bearbeiten, zweifelhaften und unterschobenen Kompositionen* (D6.251).   Works listed in this catalog are usually given with a "K" (for Köchel) number, as "Ave verum corpus, K. 620;" the works in this catalog are arranged in the order in which they were thought to be composed, without consideration as to their format.   In turn, Wolfgang Schmieder compiled *Thematisch-systematisches Verzeichnis der musikalischen Werke von Johann Sebastian Bach: Bach-Werke-Verzeichnis (BWV)* (D6.28). The works in this catalog are cited with either an "S" number (for Wolfgang Schmieder) or a "BWV" number for Bach-Werke-Verzeichnis; most authorities prefer the latter designation; in contrast to the Köchel catalog, the Bach works are listed in order by format, with vocal works coming before instrumental ones and solo and smaller ensembles listed before larger ones.   These catalogs give a great deal of information about the individual works, starting, usually with the date of composition and the location of the original manuscript (if such survives) and going on to list early editions and arrangements, as well as scholarly commentary.

The collected works of composers and the various major monuments of music are given detailed listings in two useful sources.   George R. Hill and Norris L. Stephens have recently compiled *Collected Editions, Historical Series & Sets, & Monuments of Music: A Bibliography* . The pioneer in this type of listing, Anna Harriet Heyer, edited *Historical Sets, Collected Editions, and Monuments of Music: A Guide to Their Contents* (B417; D5.511); her work gives detailed access to the multi-volume sets of scholarly editions of the major composers' work, that most libraries will classify in M3 (Library of Congress classification) or 780.9 (Dewey classification). The location of these composers' compositions in the most scholarly editions is also usually given in the individual composers' works lists, found in their articles in *The New Grove Dictionary of Music and Musicians.*

DIRECTORIES

0.65   *The Directory of Music Faculties in Colleges and Universities, U. S. and Canada, 1970.* Binghamton, N.Y.: College Music Society, 1967- .

0.66   Uscher, Nancy. *The Schirmer Guide to Schools of Music and Conservatories throughout the World.* xlii + 635 pp. New York: Schirmer Books; London: Collier Macmillan, 1988.

0.67   *Musical America: International Directory of the Performing Arts, 1993- .* New York: K-III Directory Corp., 1994- .

0.68   *Billboard International Buyer's Guide,* 1970-71- . New York: Billboard Publications, 1970- .

Another useful category of reference work is the directory, which gives location information (generally address and telephone/fax numbers) for an alphabetically-arranged list of sources in various specialties. *The Directory of Music Faculties in Colleges and Universities, U.S. and Canada* (D11.23) has been published every two years by the College Music Society (CMS) since 1967; this directory, primarily arranged by college or university and subdivided by state (arranged alphabetically by postal abbreviation), gives the full- and part-time faculties for each institution, as well as the degrees given by each institution, the address and telephone number, and the individual specialty (instrument and subjects taught), faculty rank, and highest degree held; there are indexes by specialty, so that, for instance, the voice faculty nationwide is listed in a single alphabet. (CMS also maintains a website at [http://www.music.org]) A more international approach can be found in Nancy Uscher's *The Schirmer Guide to Schools of Music and Conservatories throughout the World* (D11.60) which describes over 750 educational institutions teaching music, although individual faculty members are not included.

Musical America: International Directory of the Performing Arts (D11.45) is published annually and lists classical artists currently on the concert stage and identifies their management. Intended as a tool for those active in the world of art music, there are also listings of the principal dance and opera companies, choral groups, festivals, music schools, contests, foundations and awards, publishers, professional organizations, managers, and magazines and trade papers. And, finally, *The Billboard International Buyers' Guide* is another annually published directory, listing by company contact information for those working in the recording industry, with job titles, addresses, and telephone and fax numbers.

1

Dictionaries, Encyclopedias, Related Sources

DICTIONARIES AND ENCYCLOPEDIAS FOR OPERA

1.1   Adam, Nicky, editor. *Who's Who in British Opera.* 339 pp. Aldershot, England: Scholar Press; Brookfield, Vt.: Ashgate Publishing Company, 1993.

Provides information on nearly 500 people involved with opera at the time of publication. Appendixes are included for subjects, operas and composers, record labels.

1.2   Anderson, James. *Dictionary of Opera and Operetta.* 2nd edition. 656 pp. London: Bloomsbury, 1995.

Useful for any reader, but geared towards a younger operatic audience, the writing style is a bit more personal and subjective than most dictionaries. Expansive range including entries for festivals, literary sources, characters and related voice types, vocal ranges, an operatic chronology organized by country and also a discography. Readers should note that it was first published as the *Bloomsbury Dictionary of Opera and Operetta* in 1989 and reprinted as *The Complete Dictionary of Opera and Operetta* in 1993 by Wings Books (New York).

1.3   Bagnoli, Giorgio. *The La Scala Encyclopedia of the Opera.* Translated by Graham Fawcett. 398 pp. New York: Simon & Schuster, 1993.

Includes entries for nearly 500 operas as well as more than 800 people. Many illustrations, but no clue as to its connection to La Scala. First published in Italy by A. Mondadori in 1993 under the title *Opera.*

1.4   Benford, Harry. *The Gilbert and Sullivan Lexicon; In Which is Gilded the Philosophic Pill.* Second edition; revised and enlarged. 270 pp. Ann Arbor, Mich. : Sarah Jennings Press, 1991.

Arranged chronologically by operetta, and then, for the terms themselves, arranged as each term first appears in the work. Full of drawings, and written very much in the G&S spirit, quite entertaining while at the same time, clarifying the meaning behind such things as an "Italian glance" and "furbelow."

1.5   Davis, Peter G. *The American Opera Singer: The Lives and Adventures of America's Great Singers in Opera and Concert, from 1825 to the Present.* 626 pp. New York: Doubleday, 1997.

An interesting book with plenty of photographs and a fairly extensive bibliography.

1.6   Fitzgerald, Gerald, editor-in-chief. *Annals of the Metropolitan Opera: The Complete Chronicle of Performances and Artists.* 2 vols. Boston: G. K. Hall, 1990.

Provides comprehensive, factual information about the Met's seasons from October 1883 to June 1985. Its forerunner, *Metropolitan Opera Annals*, was published in 1947. The first volume of the present edition chronicles every performance by season, whether at the opera house or elsewhere. Each season includes an introduction, list of the season's repertory, personnel roster and the chronology of performances. The second volume is a collection of tables: performances, subdivided by operas, dances works, concert works, other performances; composers and librettists, each treated separately; production artists, subdivided by directors, designers, choreographers; performing artists, subdivided by conductors, vocal artists, dancers, other performers, guest appearances; performance locations; broadcast performances; and translations, subdivided by works in translations and translators. Four appendixes list chief administrators, chorus masters, ballet masters, and world and U.S. premieres. There are numerous photographs.

1.7   Gammond, Peter. *An Illustrated Guide to Composers of Opera.* 240 pp. London: Salamander; New York: Arco, 1980.

Brief biographies of over 100 composers of opera, which were previously published in *The Illustrated Encyclopedia of Recorded Opera* (5.7), along with lists of their operas and some accompanying information.   Many photographs and color reproductions of portraits.

1.8   Griffel, Margaret Ross.   *Operas in German: A Dictionary.*   735 pp. Westport, Conn.:   Greenwood Press, 1990.

Lists approximately 380 operas written either from German sources or from German translations. Most of the composers represented were born in German-speaking countries.   The dictionary includes six appendixes, as well as a chronology of the operas. There is also a bibliography.   A companion volume, *Operas in English: A Dictionary* is expected for publication by Greenwood Press in 1998.

1.9   Guinn, John, and Les Stone.   *St. James Opera Encyclopedia: A Guide to People and Works.*   958 pp.   Detroit, Mich.:   Visible Ink Press, 1997.

Signed articles on, as the title implies, people and works. There is a title index, but no index for people.   There is, however a biographical index for the more than 150 contributing writers.

1.10   Hamilton, David, editor.   *The Metropolitan Opera Encyclopedia: A Comprehensive Guide to the World of Opera.*   415 pp.   New York: Simon & Schuster; Metropolitan Opera Guild, 1987.

A basic encyclopedic format on the opera, but interestingly interspersed with "guest essays" written by opera singers, critics, and scholars.   There is a chronology and list of suggested readings as well as many photographs, some in color.

1.11   Hamilton, Mary.   *A - Z of Opera.*   223 pp.   New York: Facts on File, 1990.

Geared towards those new to opera. Basis of selection for entries has been based on those operas considered to be in the core repertoire of British and American opera.

1.12   Holden, Amanda, Nicholas Kenyon, and Stephen Walsh. *The Viking Opera Guide*. 1,305 pp. and CD-ROM. London; New York: Viking, 1993.

A directory to more than 800 composers and their operas by approximately 100 contributing writers. Entries are signed with contributors' initials. Term glossary and an appendix listing librettists are included. Selective videographies and discographies accompany the opera entries. There is also an abridged version by the same editors, *The Penguin Opera Guide*, published in 1995. Consisting of some 150 articles, this newer, more compact edition includes a glossary, and a biographical index to the contributors, along with indexes to librettists and titles.

1.13   LaRue, C. Steven. *International Dictionary of Opera*. 2 vols. London: St. James Press, 1993.

Approximately 1,100 signed entries. Each volume contains a "list of entries" in the prefatory pages, arranged by category (composers, conductors, librettists, performers, titles, etc.) There is a title index and a nationality index at the back of the second volume.

1.14   Loewenberg, Alfred. *Annals of Opera, 1597-1940, Compiled from the Original Sources*. 3rd edition, revised and corrected by Harold Rosenthal. xxv + 1,756 columns. Totowa, N. J.: Rowman and Littlefield; London: J. Calder, 1978.

The first edition was published by W. Heffer (Cambridge, England, 1943). The second revised and corrected edition by Societas Bibliographica (Geneva, Switzerland, 1955) was reprinted by Rowman and Littlefield in 1970 and by Scholarly Press in 1972. A long-standing valuable resource, it is divided into two parts: the first is a chronological listing of over 4,000 operas. Entries include composer and librettist, original title, place and date of first performances. The second part is a title/composer/librettist index and there is an index for subjects, places, and other terms.

1.15   Northouse, Cameron. *Twentieth Century Opera in England and the United States*. 400 pp. Boston: G. K. Hall, 1976.

Covers the years 1900 to 1974. One listing of premieres, one listing of operas having no known premiere date. Appendix A lists operas based on literary works and Appendix B lists published operas.

1.16   Orrey, Leslie. *The Encyclopedia of Opera.* 376 pp. New York: Charles Scribner's Sons, 1976.

Standard encyclopedic form, signed articles. Attention should be paid to the introduction and its rich listing of other operatic resources.

1.17   Osborne, Charles. *The Dictionary of the Opera.* 382 pp. New York: Simon & Schuster, 1983.

Lists entries for some 300 composers, 800 singers and other related personnel, brief synopses of 570 operas and includes 150 pictures. Osborne, the sole author of this dictionary, has written numerous other books on the opera, including studies on Verdi, Wagner, Puccini, and the *bel canto* operas of Rossini, Donizetti and Bellini.

1.18   Parker, Roger. *The Oxford History of Opera.* 390 pp. New York: Oxford University Press, 1996.

Twelve chapters, written by acknowledged scholars, divided into three sections (staging, singers, social climate). Also included is a "Further Reading" essay; a chronology compiled by Mary Ann Smart; and information on the contributors. Readers will note that the earlier edition (1994) is entitled *The Oxford Illustrated History of Opera.*

1.19   Rich, Maria F. *Who's Who in Opera: An International Biographical Directory of Singers, Conductors, Directors, Designers, and Administrators, also Including Profiles of 101 Opera Companies.* xxi + 684 pp. New York: Arno Press, 1976.

Information on the personnel, repertoire, and budgets from 144 opera companies. Listing of agents is also included.

1.20   Sadie, Stanley. *History of Opera.* 485 pp. London: The Macmillan Press Ltd., 1989. (The New Grove Handbooks in Music)

Partly taken from *The New Grove Dictionary of Music and Musicians* and partly newly-written, the text covers all aspects of opera and its history. Numerous contributing writers, lengthy glossary and substantial bibliography, index.

1.21   Sadie, Stanley. *New Grove Book of Operas.* 758 pp. New York: St. Martin's Press, 1997.

Also published in 1996 by Macmillan (London). A comprehensive single-volume reference source for opera, including synopses and historical background for over 250 works, a thorough glossary, indexes for both role names and first lines.

1.22   Sadie, Stanley, and Christina Bashford. *The New Grove Dictionary of Opera.* 4 vols. London: Macmillan; New York: Grove's Dictionaries of Music, 1992.

More than 1,000 writers contributed to this operatic encyclopedia. As with all the New Grove family of dictionaries, the articles are signed and include bibliographies. The *NGO* includes entries for virtually anything relating to opera. There are indexes of role names and of incipits.

1.23   Smith, Eric Ledell. *Blacks in Opera: An Encyclopedia of People and Companies, 1873 - 1993.* 236 pp. Jefferson, N. C.: McFarland, 1995.

Biographical information, along with other pertinent information about more than 500 African Americans who have been a part of the operatic world. Two appendixes list persons by occupation and by place of birth; however only page numbers are cited, not the specific person. There is an index and some photographs are scattered throughout the text.

1.24   Warrack, John, and Ewan West. *The Concise Oxford Dictionary of Opera.* 3rd edition. 571 pp. New York: Oxford University Press, 1996.

A distilled version of its larger partner volume, *The Oxford Dictionary of Opera*, this handy monograph provides a great deal of information although worklists, bibliographies and other secondary features are excluded. Following the same format as the larger volume, cross-references are indicated by an asterisk.

1.25   Warrack, John, and Ewan West. *The Oxford Dictionary of Opera*. 782 pp. New York: Oxford University Press, 1992.

A single-volume dictionary providing brief definitions and descriptions of terms, arias, operas, singers, conductors, opera houses, theaters, and place names. Cross-references are indicated by an asterisk.   Includes a brief but useful bibliography (pp. ix-xiii) which includes guidebooks and national histories of opera. Incorporates selected works lists, writings, and brief bibliographies with some entries. Includes titles in common usage (e.g., "Bell Song," "The Bartered Bride").

DICTIONARIES AND ENCYCLOPEDIAS FOR MUSICAL THEATER

1.26   Block, Geoffrey Holden. *Enchanted Evenings: The Broadway Musical from Showboat to Sondheim*. 410 pp. New York: Oxford University Press, 1997.

Examines the issues behind the success and popularity of fourteen musicals and separately in the stage works of Stephen Sondheim. Full of musical examples, photographs and Hirshfeld drawings. Included also is a discography, numerous appendixes, and a selective bibligraphy.

1.27   Bloom, Ken. *American Song: The Complete Musical Theatre Companion, Second Edition, 1877 - 1995*.   2 vols.   New York: Schirmer Books, 1996.

First edition published in 1985 by Facts on File.   Provides information on over 4,800 American musicals.   The first section lists all shows alphabetically and the second part is an index to over 70,000 songs and 27,000 artists.   There is also a chronological listing of titles.

1.28   Bloom, Ken. *Hollywood Song: The Complete Film & Musical Companion*. 3 vols. New York: Facts on File, 1995.

Information on some 7,000 foreign and American films, following a similar format to the author's *American Song* (1.27).

1.29   Bordman, Gerald. *American Musical Theatre: A Chronicle*. 2nd ed. 821 pp. New York: Oxford University Press, 1992.

Beginning with the origins of the American musical theater (before *The Black Crook* in 1866) and ending with shows appearing in 1990, the author provides an exhaustive account of the development of the genre. There are three large indexes: 'Shows and sources;' 'Songs;' 'People.' Some other titles by Bordman include *American Operetta from "HMS Pinafore" to "Sweeney Todd"* (Oxford, 1981); *American Musical Comedy from "Adonis" to "Dreamgirls"* (Oxford, 1982); and *American Musical Revue from "The Passing Show" to "Sugar Babies"* (Oxford, 1985).

1.30   Gänzl, Kurt. *The British Musical Theatre*. 2 vols. London: Macmillan, 1986.

This definitive study spans the history of the British musical stage from 1865 to 1984, the focus being on light musical theater, and not opera. There are repertoire listings for each year that include copious information about the productions.

1.31   Gänzl, Kurt. *The Encyclopedia of the Musical Theatre*. 2 vols. New York: Schirmer Books, 1994.

Almost 3,000 entries on the people and shows from those countries most heavily involved with the production of musical theater over the last 150 years, including France, Austria, Britain, Hungary and the United States.

1.32   Gänzl, Kurt. *The Musical: A Concise History*. 432 pp. Boston: Northeastern University Press, 1997.

An overview of mainstream musical theater and its international history. Includes many illustrations and the reader will find, interspersed throughout the commentary, and in bold type, background information on the musicals themselves.

1.33   Green, Stanley. *Broadway Musicals: Show by Show.* 4th edition, revised and updated by Kay Green. 372 pp. Milwaukee, Wisc.: Hal Leonard Publishing Co., 1994.

First published in 1985 by Hal Leonard Books, with intermediate editions published in 1987 by Hal Leonard and Faber (London) and in 1990 by Hal Leonard. Chronological listing of shows from 1866 (*The Black Crook*) to 1985 (*Big River*). Seven indexes: show, composer/lyricist, librettist, director, choreographer, major cast members, and theater. Entries for around 300 productions, over 100 photographs. Also included are original cast lists, songs and number of performances on Broadway and at which theater, background information. Readers should also consult the author's companion volume *Hollywood Musicals, Year by Year* (Hal Leonard, 1995).

1.34   Green, Stanley. *Encyclopedia of the Musical Theatre: An Updated Reference Guide to over 2,000 Performers, Writers, Directors, Productions, and Songs of the Musical Stage, Both in New York and London.* 492 pp. New York: Da Capo Press, 1984.

Originally published by Dodd, Mead in 1976. There is also a paperback edition (Oxford, 1988). An encyclopedic listing of all aspects of the most significant people, shows and songs of the musical theater up to the date of publication. It does not include entries for Gilbert & Sullivan, one-acts, revues, and so forth. Emphasis is placed on those shows appearing on both the New York and London stages. There is a listing of awards and prizes (Pulitzer, New York Drama Critics Circle Award, Tony) as well as one for long-running shows. Included also is a bibliography and a discography. Readers should also consult Green's companion volume, *Encyclopaedia of the Musical Film* (Oxford, 1981.)

1.35   Green, Stanley. *Rodgers and Hammerstein Fact Book: A Record of Their Work Together and with Other Collaborators.* 762 + 32 pp. New York: Drama Book Specialists, 1981.

Published previously as *The Richard Rodgers Fact Book* (1965). Information on the two, both separately and as a team. There are fact sheets about each and chronological listings of shows. Pertinent information of all sorts is included about each production as well as a listing of songs arranged by category (e.g. age, colors, family, holidays, kisses, moon, etc.).

1.36   Hischak, Thomas S. *Stage It with Music: An Encyclopedic Guide to the American Musical Theatre.* 341 pp. Westport, Conn.: Greenwood Press, 1993.

Short entries for over 300 shows, along with performers, composers, lyricists, designers, choreographers, and so on. There is also a chronological listing of musicals from 1866 through 1992, a selective bibliography, and a thorough index.

1.37   Hischak, Thomas S. *The American Musical Theatre Song Encyclopedia.*   543 pp. Westport, Conn.: Greenwood Press, 1995.

Included are approximately 1800 songs written for the stage as early as 1966 and as late as the 1993-94 theater season. Emphasis is on American musical theater although others will be found (not Gilbert & Sullivan however). The entries include a description of the song, the name of the character(s) singing it, the name of the actor, the show and date of premiere.

1.38   Mandelbaum, Ken. *Not Since Carrie; Forty Years of Broadway Flops.* 372 pp. New York: St. Martin's Press, 1991.

An examination of some of the shows that didn't make it, ranging from 1950 to 1990, including the musical version of Stephen King's *Carrie.* The shows included ran no more than 250 performances. Many photographs are included. Some titles can also be found in Richard Lynch's *Musicals!* (7.19)

1.39   Peterson, Bernard L. *A Century of Musicals in Black and White: An Encyclopedia of Musical Stage Works by, about, or involving African Americans.* 529 pp. Westport, Conn.: Greenwood Press, 1993.

Provides information on over 1200 works for the musical stage that involve, African-Americans. It is a companion volume to two others by the same author: *Contemporary Black American Playwrights and their Plays: a Biographical Directory and Dramatic Index* (1988) and *Early Black American Playwrights and Dramatic Writers: a Biographical Directory and Catalog of Plays, Films, and*

Broadcasting Scripts (1990). Included is a chronology of the shows, name index, song index, general index, and a listing of information sources.

1.40   Simas, Rick. *The Musicals No One Came to See: A Guidebook to Four Decades of Musical-Comedy Casualties on Broadway, Off-Broadway and in Out-of-Town Try-Out, 1943-1983.*   639   pp. New York: Garland, 1987.   (Garland Reference Library of the Humanities, 563)

Lists those shows that ran less than 300 performances or closed during try-outs. Includes an appendix for opening dates, a show title index and two for sources and related authors; librettists, composers and lyricists. One interesting aspect of the book is to identify shows which failed at first but were successful in revival, such as *Pal Joey.*

1.41   Suskin, Steven. *Show Tunes, 1905-1991: The Songs, Shows and Careers of Braodway's Major Composers.*   769 pp.   Revised and expanded edition. New York: Limelight Editions, 1992. (New York)

First published in 1986 by Dodd, Mead.   Thirty composers and their shows, listed in chronological order. There is a list of collaborators, a bibliography, and indexes to both song and show titles, and to people.   Two other interesting volumes by the same author are *Opening Night on Broadway* and *More Opening Nights on Broadway* (Schirmer Books, 1990 and 1997, respectively).   Both are quotebooks of reviews for shows running from 1943 to 1964 in the former and 1965 to 1981 in the latter.

RELATED SOURCES

1.42   Barber, Josephine. *German for Musicians.*   277 pp.   Bloomington: Indiana University Press, 1985.

A highly useful book for any musician needing to improve language skills in German. The book is designed as a textbook equivalent to one academic year's study, with twenty lessons which are located in parts one and two, each ending with a poem taken from the Lieder repertory.   The third part contains further practice readings, each increasingly difficult.   Part 4 is a reference section including such topics as musical vocabulary, examples of opera contracts and application letters, the Gothic alphabet, a grammar summary as well as an index of grammer, answers to the exercises included in the text, information about the authors cited in the text and a bibliography.

1.43   Reid, Cornelius L. *A Dictionary of Vocal Terminology: An Analysis.* xxi + 457 pp. New York: Joseph Patelson Music House, 1983.

The author lists his objectives for the dictionary as follows: "1) foster a more perceptive insight into natural functioning and the principles which govern that process; 2) make those terms introduced by scientists more familiar and understandable to students, singers, and teachers of voice; 3) acquaint scientists with the significance and etymology of vocal terms from the perspective of the voice teacher; and 4) provide a basis upon which a standard terminology can evolve which will strike a balance between aesthetics and natural functioning." (p. xxi) There is an index of terms in the prefatory pages and an index to names and a bibliography at the back. Some illustrations included. "See" references are noted in the margins.

1.44   Risatti, Howard. *New Music Vocabulary: A Guide to Notational Signs for Contemporary Music.* 219 pp. Urbana, Ill.: University of Illinois Press, 1975.

Divided into six chapters, the last of which deals with the voice. Defines terms and gives examples of related symbols. The first chapter, "General Notational Material" is also useful for singers. List of cited works, bibliography and index are included. A similiar source, equally dated, is *The Language of Twentieth Century Music: A Dictionary of Terms* by Robert Fink and Robert Ricci, published by Schirmer Books, also in 1975.

1.45   Yarbrough, Julie. *Modern Languages for Musicians.*   499 pp. Stuyvesant, NY: Pendragon Press, 1993.

A handbook on German, French and Italian grammar and pronunciation. There is no index, but the table of contents clearly delineates each chapter.

2

Guides to Repertoire and Research

SOLO AND CHAMBER

2.1   Bayne, Pauline Shaw, and Patricia Barkelow. *Song Index: University of Tennessee at Knoxville.* 30 microfiche and accompanying booklet. Knoxville, Tenn.: University of Tennessee Library, 1981.

Indexs 554 anthologies and songbooks.   Also available on the Internet [http://toltec.lib.utk.edu/~music/music-songlist-home.html].

2.2   Berry, Corre.   *Vocal Chamber Duets: An Annotated Bibliography.* 71 pp. National Association of Teachers of Singing, 1981.

Lists duets by some 105 composers in eighty-eight collections. Indexes include accompaniments with instruments other than keyboard, voice combinations, composers, poets, and title/first line.

2.3   Brunnings, Florence E. *Folk Song Index: A Comprehensive Guide to the Florence E. Brunnings Collection.* lxxxi + 372 pp. New York: Garland Publishing, 1981. (Garland reference library of the humanities, 252)

Indexes over 1,300 anthologies in both print and sound.

2.4   Carman, Judith E. *Art-Song in the United States 1801-1976: An Annotated Bibliography.* 2nd ed., and enl. 308 pp. Jacksonville, Fla.: National Association of Teachers of Singing, 1987. With a special section: *Art-Song in the United States 1759-1810* by Gordon Myers.

First published in 1976. Devised as a resource for voice teachers and college-level students and above. Four considerations outlined selection criteria for the bibliography: an aid in vocal development; useful for programming of recitals; overall quality of the song; and historical purposes. Each entry includes title, poet, publication data, dedications, key or tonality (or lack thereof) range and tessitura, meter and tempo; length, level of difficulty for both singer and accompanist; voice type; mood and subject; description the song; special difficulty; and uses. Appendixes are included for additional listings, publishers, and sample recital programs of American song. There are indexes for subject-poet, composer and title.

2.5   Dunlap, Kay and Barbara Winchester. *Vocal Chamber Music.* 140 pp. New York: Garland Publishing, Inc., 1985. (Garland reference library of the humanities; vol. 465)

Arranged alphabetically by composer, this volume lists chamber pieces scored for as few as one voice and one instrument (other than piano or guitar) up to twelve solo voices and twelve instruments and covers a time frame of 1650 to 1980. The works themselves are arranged alphabetically or, where applicable, by opus number. The index is arranged by scoring (e.g. S, db, vib).

2.6   Espina, Noni. *Repertoire for the Solo Voice: A Fully Annotated Guide to Works for the Solo Voice Published in Modern Editions and Covering Material from the 13th Century to the Present.* 2 vols. Metuchen, N. J.: The Scarecrow Press, 1977.

Listings for art songs, arias, traditional songs, and florid songs, arranged by nationality of the composer. Information given on style and vocal needs for each selection. Indexes to sources and composers.

2.7   Ferguson, Gary Lynn. *Song Finder: A Title Index to 32,000 Popular Songs in Collection, 1854-1992.* 344 pp. Westport, Conn.: Greenwood Press, 1995. (Music Reference Collection, 46)

Access by song title only to 621 songbooks found in the State Library of Louisiana, more than 75% of which have never been indexed elsewhere.

2.8   Fitch, Donald. *Blake Set to Music: A Bibliography of Musical Settings of the Poems and Prose of William Blake.* xxix + 281 pp. Berkeley, Calif.: University of California Press, 1989. (University of California publications. Catalogs and bibliographies, 5)

Listed alphabetically by composer, includes more than 1,400 works.

2.9   Goleeke, Thomas. *Literature for the Voice: An Index of Songs in Collections and Source Book for Teachers of Singing.* 223 pp. Metuchen, N. J.: The Scarecrow Press, Inc., 1984.

Geared towards teachers with beginning students and for those who teach class voice. The book includes chapters on class voice, a listing of collections, a bibliography of important sources and, most importantly, includes the ranges for each song and the language(s) of the texts. The collections listed, sixty in all, are the standards that have long been used in the studio including *The New Imperial Edition* series, *The Singing Road*, and *24 Italian Art Songs and Arias.* Indexes for song titles and composers are included.

2.10   Gooch, Bryan N. S., David S. Thatcher and Odean Long. *Musical Settings of British Romantic Literature: A Catalogue.* 2 vols. New York: Garland Publishing, 1982. (Garland reference library of the humanities, 326)

Both published and unpublished musical settings of British authors who were born after 1750. Arranged alphabetically by author and literary work. Indexes for authors, first lines/titles, and composers.

2.11   Gooch, Bryan N. S., David S. Thatcher and Odean Long. *Musical Settings of Early and Mid-Victorian Literature: A Catalogue.* xxxvi + 946 pp. New York: Garland Publishing, 1979. (Garland reference library of the humanities, 149)

Both published and unpublished musical settings of British authors who were born after 1800. Same format as 2.10.

2.12   Gooch, Bryan N. S., David S. Thatcher and Odean Long. *Musical Settings of Late Victorian and Modern British Literature: A Catalogue.* xxiii + 1,112 pp. New York: Garland Publishing, 1976. (Garland reference library of the humanities, 31)

Same format as 2.10

2.13   Gooch, Bryan and David S. Thatcher. *A Shakespeare Music Catalogue.*
        5 vols. Oxford: Clarendon Press, 1991.

Lists over 21,000 works. There are indexes for titles of Shakespeare's works;
musical works; and composers, arrangers, and librettists. A list of publishers is
also included.

2.14   Goodfellow, William D.   *Wedding Music: An Index to Collections.*
        197 pp.   Metuchen, N. J. and London: The Scarecrow Press, Inc.,
        1992.

Indexes almost two hundred collections of wedding music, most of them vocal
music. In all, the index lists more than 3,400 pieces. Arranged in four parts:
list of books indexed (with the OCLC number thoughtfully included); title/first
line index; composer index; instrumental music index. Goodfellow, a reference
librarian, has also compiled *Where's That Tune?: An Index to Songs in
Fakebooks* (Scarecrow, 1990).

2.15   Havlice. Patricia. *Popular Song Index.*   933 pp.   Metuchen, N. J.:
        The Scarecrow Press, 1975.

With the first supplement published in 1978, the second in 1984, and the third
in 1989. Indexes the songs found in 710 anthologies published since 1940.

2.16   Hovland, Michael.   *Musical Settings of American Poetry;   a
        Bibliography.*   531 pp.   New York: Greenwood Press, 1986.
        (Music reference collection, no. 8)

Guides the reader to 5,800 musical settings written by 2,100 composers on
2,400 titles for texts written by some ninety-nine American authors. In addition
to citing the various settings, the compiler indicates anthologies and song
collections where the songs can be located. Indexes of composers and titles of
the literary works.

2.17   Klaus, Kenneth S. *Chamber Music for Solo Voice and Instruments,
        1960 -1989: An Annotated Guide.* 222 pp. Berkeley, CA: Fallen Leaf
        Press, 1994. (Fallen Leaf reference books in music, 29)

Arranged by voice type, the guide provides a listing of over 700 chamber works by more than 500 composers. Each entry includes language and source of text, instrumentation, the vocal range and the level of difficulty, along with date of composition, publisher, and so forth. Readers should take note of a newer similar volume by James F. Maroney which was just recently published in 1997. Its title is *Music for Voice and Classical Guitar, 1945-1996: An Annotated Catalog* (McFarland).

2.18   Lowenberg, Carlton. *Musicians Wrestle Everywhere: Emily Dickinson and Music.* 210 pp. Berkeley, Calif.: Fallen Leaf Press, 1992. (Fallen Leaf reference books in music, 19)

Lists both solo and ensemble compositions by 276 composers.

2.19   Lust, Patricia. *American Vocal Chamber Music, 1945 - 1980.* 273 pp. Westport, Conn.: Greenwood Press, 1985. (Music reference collection, no. 4)

An annotated bibliography comprised of 544 entries for music written for one or two voices and up to fifteen instruments, excluding works for voice and keyboard. The bibliography is preceded by an essay entitled "Observations of Trends" which discusses new styles of notation, dynamics, uses of instruments and so forth. Three appendixes reorganize the bibliography by voice and instrument; number of performers; type of ensemble. There is an index of titles as well as a general index.

2.20   Manning, Jane. *New Vocal Repertory; An Introduction.* 284 pp. Basingstoke: Macmillan Press, 1986.

A type of graded list of "new" English-language music, categorized by technical difficulty, ranging from a level I to a level VI, as designated by the author. Criteria for selection is based on accessibility by those singers not necessarily considered to be specialists or virtuosos within the realm of new music, in hopes of introducing these works into the repertoire. A listing of publishers' addresses will be found within the Acknowledgements and there is a composer index.

2.21   Nardone, Thomas R. *Classical Vocal Music in Print.* 650 pp. Philadelphia, Pa.: Musicdata, 1976. (Music in print series, 4)

Alphabetically arranged by composer. Lists currently-available scores as reported by publishers. Additional volumes published are the *1985 Supplement* (Gary S. Eslinger, editor), the *1995 Supplement* (F. Mark Daugherty, editor) and the *Master Index 1995*.

2.22   Ord, Alan J. *Songs for Bass Voice: An Annotated Guide to Works for Bass Voice.* 218 pp. Metuchen, N. J. and London: The Scarecrow Press, Inc., 1994.

A practical graded list of repertoire for bass voice, compiled by an active teacher/performer. By arranging the guide into thirteen chapters and by including four useful appendixes, the author provides an easy-to-use resource. Annotations include a great deal of information, most importantly the range and tessitura of the piece and the level of difficulty.

2.23   Peters, Erskine. *Lyrics of the Afro-American Spiritual: A Documentary Collection.* xxxi + 463 pp. Westport, Conn.: Greenwood, 1993. (Greenwood Encyclopedia of Black Music)

Lyrics of the spirituals are separated into 9 categories. Geared towards historians and theologians, but still useful for singers as it includes sources for the texts, many of which are collections of spirituals and folk songs. There is also a selected bibliography of song collections and books on history and interpretation. Extended essay on the historical background of the Afro-American spiritual. Indexes included.

2.24   Pilkington, Michael. *Campion, Dowland and the Lutenist Songwriters.* 179 pp. London: Duckworth, 1989. (English solo song: guides to the repertoire)

One of three volumes currently available in this series, which is planned to cover the whole of the English song repertoire. The four other volumes are *Gurney, Ireland, Quilter and Warlock* (Duckworth, 1989), *Delius, Bridge and Somervell* (Thames, 1993). *Purell* and *Parry and Stanford* (Thames, 1994 and 1997 respectively). Also published by Thankes in 1997, is the author's *English Solo Song*, a valuable volume which lists, as stated in his subtitle, "a guide for singers, teachers, librarians and the music trade of songs currently available. Thorough annotations and appropriate indexes make this a useful series for the studio.

2.25   Snyder, Lawrence D. *German Poetry in Song; An Index of Lieder.* 730
        pp. Berkeley, CA: Fallen Leaf Press, 1995. (Fallen Leaf Reference
        Books in Music, 30)   *Index of Composers' Titles: Supplement.*
        197 pp.

Arranged by poet, this volume indexes more than 9,800 Lieder. Leads the reader
to the compositions of 370 composers and over 1,100 poets.

2.26   Stewart-Green, Miriam. *Women Composers: A Checklist of Works for
        the Solo Voice.* 297 pp. Boston: G. K. Hall & Co., 1980.

A listing of works by 3,736 women composers.

2.27   Studwell, William E. *Christmas Carols: A Reference Guide.* Indexes
        by David A. Hamilton, 278 pp. New York: Garland Publishing,
        1985.

Alphabetical listing of nearly 800 carols. Titles are given in original language,
easily traced in the title index. There is also a chronology of carols, a
bibliography, and a section providing general information on the genre.

2.28   Swanekamp, Joan.   *English Ayres; A Selectively Annotated
        Bibliography and Discography.* 141 pp. Westport, Conn.: Greenwood
        Press, 1984.

Offers extensive bibliographical materials on twenty-seven composers of this
genre (e.g. Campion, Dowland, Morley, Rosseter) as well as on the ayre itself.
Each entry is divided by reading materials, first editions, facsimiles, later
editions, collections and works published individually, in that order. There is
both an author and a title index.

2.29   Villamil, Victoria Etnier. *A Singer's Guide to the American Art Song,
        1870-1980.* xxi + 452 pp. Metuchen, N. J.: The Scarecrow Press,
        Inc., 1993.

Arranged alphabetically by composer, provides information on some 150
American composers of art song (twenty-one women composers included) and
their songs, although it is not necessarily a complete list of song titles for each
composer. Entries for each composer include biographiphical information,
background information on the songs, publication and recording information, the

songs themselves, publication and descriptive information, and timings. The compiler, herself a singer, states in the introduction that in some cases, those songs included are based on her personal recommendations and that some lists are complete and some are not. There is a Foreword written by Thomas Hampson. There is a supplementary song list in an Appendix. A second Appendix lists the contents of twenty-seven anthologies that include American art songs. A third lists publishers addresses and phone numbers. There is a bibliography, a brief discography, and indexes to song titles and poets.

2.30   Whaples, Miriam K. *Bach Aria Index.* 88 pp. Ann Arbor, Mich: Music Library Association, 1971. (MLA index series, 11)

Access to arias is arranged by instrumentation. There is a first-line index.

OPERA AND MUSICAL THEATER

2.31   Boldrey, Richard. *Guide to Operatic Duets.* 130 pp. Dallas, Tex.: Pst, ...Inc., 1994.

Lists all the duets found in the standard operatic repertoire, listed by role, title and voice type. There are indexes by opera title and by composer.

2.32   Boldrey, Richard. *Guide to Operatic Roles & Arias.* 554 pp. Dallas, Tex.: Pst..., Inc., 1994.

Provides roles and arias for more than 1,000 operas. Indexed by voice type, composer, and opera.

2.33   Borroff, Edith. *American Operas: A Checklist.* 334 pp. Warren, Mich.: Harmonie Park Press, 1992. (Detroit studies in music bibliography; no. 69)

A listing of some 4,000 operas by 2,000 composers. Includes, where available, performance length, first performance date and location, publisher and also includes lists of sources cited and publishers' addresses.

2.34   Lewine, Richard and Alfred Simon. *Songs of the Theater.* 897 pp. New York: H. W. Wilson Co., 1984.

Previous editions include *Encyclopedia of Theatre Music: A Comprehensive Listing of More than 4000 Songs from Broadway and Hollywood, 1900-1960*, published in 1961 by Random House and *Songs of the American Theater: A Comprehensive Listing of More than 12,000 Songs, including Selected Titles from film and Television Productions*, published in 1973 by Dodd, Mead. The present edition lists approximately 17,000 songs performed in musicals both on and off Broadway between the years 1891 and 1983. Also included is a chronology of stage productions, an index to film and television productions, and an index to composers, lyricists, and authors.

2.35 Pallay, Steven G. *Cross Index Title Guide to Opera and Operetta.* 214 pp. New York: Greenwood Press, 1989. (Music reference collection, 19)

Lists 5,500 excerpts from more than 1,400 works by 535 composers.

SACRED VOCAL

2.36 Brusse, Corre Berry. *Sacred Vocal Duets: An Annotated Bibliography.* 82 pp. Jacksonville, Fla.: National Association of Teachers of Singing, 1987.

Lists 475 sacred duets. Like the author's previous bibliography, (2.2) includes indexes for accompaniments with instruments other than keyboard, voice combinations, composers, poets, and title/first line.

2.37 Dox, Thurston J. *American Oratorios and Cantatas: A Catalog of Works Written in the United States from Colonial Times to 1985.* 2 vols. Metuchen, N. J.: The Scarecrow Press, Inc., 1986.

Lists over 3,450 works by more than 1,000 composers. Divided into four large sections (oratorios, cantatas, ensemble cantatas, and choral theater), each entry offers, as available, composer and dates, title of work, publisher information, description, vocal and instrumental requirements, characters, text source, approximate performance length, page length, parts, location of score and manuscript, first performances, and reviews.

2.38 Espina, Noni. *Vocal Solos for Christian Churches: A Descriptive Reference of Solo Music for the Church Year, Including a*

Bibliographical Supplement of Choral Works. 3rd edition. 241 pp. Methuchen, N. J.: The Scarecrow Press, 1984.

First published as *Vocal Solos for Protestant Services* in 1964 and again in 1974. Indexed by occasion, voice, title, and composer.

2.39   Evans, Margaret R.   *Sacred Cantatas: An Annotated Bibliography, 1960-1979.* 188 pp. Jefferson, N. C. and London: McFarland, 1982.

Provides substantially detailed annotations for cantatas published between 1960 and 1979, written for Protestant worship and ranging from seven to thirty minutes in length.

2.40   Laster, James H.   *Catalogue of Vocal Solos and Duets Arranged in Biblical Order.* 204 pp. Metuchen, N. J. and London: The Scarecrow Press, Inc., 1984.

Each entry includes scripture reference, composer, title, accompaniment, vocal range, and publisher with most recent date of publication.

BIBLIOGRAPHIES AND MONOGRAPHS FOR RESEARCH

2.41   Banfield, Stephen. *Sensibility and English Song: Critical Studies of the Early 20th Century.* 2 vols. Cambridge; New York: Cambridge University Press, 1985

Also published as a single-volume paperback in 1988.   The author examines British song literature from 1899 with Edward Elgar's *Sea Pictures* up through the works of Benjamin Britten and   William Walton.   The second volume includes song lists for fifty-four composers. There are three appendixes, the third being a reprint of a concert review entitled "On Interpreting Housman." Extensive bibliography and index.

2.42   Cowden, Robert H. *Classical Singers of the Opera and Recital Stages: A Bibliography of Biographical Materials.* 509 pp. Westport, Conn.: Greenwood Press, 1994. (Music Reference Collection, Number 42)

This is, to quote the compiler, a "complete reworking" of his 1985 bibliography, *Concert and Opera Singers: a Bibliography of Biographical Materials* (Greenwood). It leads the reader to information on 1,532 singers in a wide variety of sources. The compiler divides the bibliography into three sections: Part A lists books on singers; Part B lists "related books" or books which are more broad in coverage but still offer biographical information on singers; and Part C lists individual singers and sources of information about them. Most useful is an index of singers found in *The New Grove Dictionary of Opera*. Cowden has also compiled *Concert and Opera Conductors: A Bibliography of Biographical Materials* published by Greenwood Press in 1987.

2.43   Donington, Robert. *The Opera*. 238 pp. New York: Harcourt Brace Jovanovich, Inc., 1978. (The Harbrace History of Musical Forms)

A well-written general overview of the history of opera by noted English musicologist Robert Donington. Includes a list for additional reading and an index. Other books about opera by this author are *The Rise of Opera* (1981), *Wagner's 'Ring' and Its Symbols* (1963, revised 1974), and *Opera and Its Symbols: the Unity of Words, Music, and Staging* (1990).

2.44   Farkas, Andrew. *Opera and Concert Singers: An Annotated International Bibliography of Books and Pamphlets.* 363 pp. New York: Garland, 1985.

As opposed to the Cowden bibliographies (2.42), this bibliography lists only monographic titles. It covers 796 singers spanning over 400 years and 1850 individual titles, published through 1983. Divided into three parts: single-subject monographs; multi-subject monographs; and manuscript sources. Each part is arranged alphabetically by singer. There is an author index

2.45   Friedberg, Ruth C. *American Art Song and American Poetry*. 3 vols. Metuchen, N.J.: The Scarecrow Press, Inc., 1981, 1984, 1987.

Examines songs written by thirty-two American composers, starting with Edward MacDowell and ending with John Corigliano. Includes Duke, Copland, Rorem, Bowles, among others.

2.46   Lakeway, Ruth C., and Robert C. White, Jr. *Italian Art Song*. 399 pp. Bloomington: Indiana University Press, 1989.

Examines the *liriche da camera*, or Italian art song, composed since around the turn of the century, which the authors define in their preface as "compositions for solo voice and piano that achieve a true synthesis of music and poetry while

utilizing the piano for its unique contribution to the totality of expression."
Translations of texts, along with suggestions for performance are included for
over 200 songs.   Some of the composers included are Respighi, Pizzetti,
Malipiero, Castelnuovo-Tedesco and Giordano.

2.47   Marco, Guy A. *Opera: A Research and Information Guide.* 373 pp.
         New York: Garland, 1984.   (Garland reference library of the
         humanities; v. 468)

This is a thorough examination of what the author labels the "core" literature for
research in opera. It includes a substantial list of reference books covering all
aspects of opera but also includes listings of resources for the study of individual
operas as well as operas from specific countries. An appendix lists over 1,000
operas, arranged by composer. The titles are in their original language, using
standardized spellings adopted by the Library of Congress.   There are two
indexes: author-title and subject.

2.48   Meares, Stan. *British Opera in Retrospect.* 149 pp.   Upminster,
         Essex: British Music Society, 1986.

Twenty-five short essays, contributed by twenty noteworthy scholars (e.g.
Stephen Banfield, Lewis Foreman, and Henry Raynor) provide on overview of
British opera, beginning with Henry Purcell up to the present day. Provides a
great deal of interesting background material, but also information on less-
familiar repertoire.

2.49   Meister, Barbara. *Art Song: The Marriage of Music and Poetry.* 231
         pp. Wakefield, N.H.: Hollowbrook Publishing, 1992.

The author takes a look at songs by Mozart, Schubert, Schumann, Brahms,
Wolf, Strauss, Duparc, Debussy, Fauré, Auric, and Copland. The text is written
more for the listener than the performer, although since some of the repertoire
discussed isn't as commonly heard as others, it offers some useful information.
There is a bibliography but no index. Other books by this author are *An
Introduction to the Art Song* (Taplinger, 1980) and *Nineteenth-century French
Song: Fauré, Chausson, Duparc and Debussy* (Indiana University Press, 1980).
Additionally, readers should consult Carol Kimball's book, *Song: A Guide to
Style and Literature* (Pst...,Inc., 1996).

2.50   Osborne, Charles. *The Concert Song Companion: A Guide to the Classical Repertoire.* 285 pp. New York: Da Capo, 1985. (A Da Capo Paperback)

Originally published by Gollancz (London) in 1974. A broad overview of art song intended for music-lovers in general.

2.51   Parsons, Charles H. *The Mellen Opera Reference Index.* 20 vols. Lewiston, N.Y.: Edwine Mellen Press, 1986-1997.

This series of indexes covers the following: composers and their works, librettists, a geographical index of premieres, subjects of operas, discographies arranged both by composers and performers, cast lists of premieres, a bibliography, and reviews and re-assessments of premiere performances.

2.52   Seaton, Douglass. *The Art Song: A Research and Information Guide.* 273 pp. New York: Garland Publishing, Inc., 1987. (Music research and information guides; vol. 6) (Garland reference library of the humanities; vol. 673)

An annotated bibliography of books, monographs, selected articles, and selected theses and dissertations. There is also an historical survey of the form. Categories include general studies, individual composers, individual poets, aesthetics, analysis, criticism, texts and translations, performance, bibliographies and sources.

2.53   Stevens, Denis. *A History of Song.* Revised edition. 491 pp. New York: Norton, 1970.

First edition published in 1960 by Hutchinson, London and in 1961 by Norton, New York. This overview approaches the history of song both historically and geographically, with all individual portions written by a variety of scholars. Understandably extensive indexes.

BIBLIOGRAPHIC RESOURCES: INDIVIDUAL COMPOSERS

2.54   *Bio-bibliographies in Music.* Greenwood Press offers this long-standing series of bibliographic guides for individual composers which all include a brief biography of the composer, a works list, a bibliography and a discography, along with any other pertinent

information. A current listing includes the following composers
(author, date of publication and series number in parentheses).

Archer, Violet. (Linda Bishop Hartig, 1991, no. 41)
Ballou, Esther Williamson. (James R. Heintze, 1987, no. 5)
Barber, Samuel. (Don A Hennessee, 1985, no. 3)
Bassett, Leslie. (Ellen S. Johnson, 1994, no. 52)
Bennett, Richard Rodney. (Stewart R. Craggs, 1990, no. 24)
Bennett, Robert Russell. (George Joseph Ferencz, 1990, no. 29)
Bliss, Arthur. (Craggs, Stewart R., 1988, no. 13)
Bridge, Frank. (Karen R. Little, 1991, no. 36)
Britain, Radie. (Walter B. Bailey, 1990, no. 25)
Busoni, Ferruccio. (Marc-André Roberge, 1995, no.34)
Carpenter, John Alden. (Joan O'Connor, 1994, no. 54)
Carter, Elliott. (William T. Doering, 1993, no. 51)
Chaminade, Cécile. (Cirton, Marcia J., 1988, no. 15)
Copland, Aaron. (JoAnn Skowronski, 1985, no.2)
Creston, Paul. (Monica J. Slomski, 1994, no. 55)
Davies, Peter Maxwell. (Carolyn J. Smith, 1995, no. 57)
Finney, Ross Lee. (Susan Hayes Hitchens, 1996, no. 63)
Finzi, Gerald. (John Clay Dressler, 1997, no. 65)
Foss, Lukas. (Karen L. Perone, 1991, no. 37)
Glanville-Hicks, Peggy. (Deborah Hayes, 1990, no. 27)
Granados, Enrique. (Carol A. Hess, 1991, no. 42)
Hanson, Howard. (James E. Perone, 1993, no. 47)
Harris, Roy. (Dan Stehman, 1991, no. 40)
Hill, Edward Burlingame. (Linda L. Tyler, 1989, no. 21)
Hoddinott, Alun. (Stewart R. Craggs, 1993, no. 44)
Husa, Karel. (Susan Hayes Hitchens, 1991, no. 31)
Ives, Charles. (Geoffrey Holden Block, 1988, no. 14)
Kay, Ulysses. (Constance Tibbs Hobson, 1994, no. 53)
Krenek, Ernst. (Garrett H. Bowles, 1989, no. 22)
Langlais, Jean. (Kathleen Thomerson, 1988, no. 10)
Ligeti, György. (Robert W. Richard, 1990, no. 30)
Luening, Otto. (Ralph Hartsock, 1991, no. 35)
Martin, Frank. (Charles W. King, 1990, no. 26)
Mason, Lowell. (Carol A. Pemberton, 1988, no. 11)
Mathias, William. (Stewart R. Craggs, 1995, no. 58)
McCabe, John. (Stewart R. Craggs, 1991, no. 32)
McKinley, William Thomas. (Jeffrey S. Sposato, 1995, no. 56)
Messager, André. (John Wagstaff, 1991, no. 33)
Milner, Anthony. (James Siddons, 1989, no. 20)
Musgrave, Thea. (Donald L. Hixon, 1984, no. 1)
Persichetti, Vincent. (Patterson, Donald L., 1988, no. 16)

Pinkham, Daniel. (Kee DeBoer, 1988, no. 12)
Poulenc, Francis. (George Russell Keck, 1990, no. 28)
Read, Gardner. (Mary Ann Dodd, 1996, no. 60)
Reger, Max. (William E. Grim, 1988, no. 7)
Rorem, Ned. (Arlys L. McDonald, 1989, no. 23)
Rosbaud, Hans. (Joan Evans, 1992, no. 43)
Roussell, Albert. (Robert Follet, 1988, no. 19)
Ruggles, Carl. (Jonathan D. Green, 1995, no. 59)
Sapp, Allen. (Allen Green, 1996, no. 62)
Sauget, Henri. (David L. Austin, 1991, no. 39)
Schuller, Gunther. (Norbert Carnovale, 1987, no. 6)
Sculthorpe, Peter. (Deborah Hayes, 1993, no. 50)
Sitsky, Larry. (Robyn Holmes, 1997, no. 64)
Still, William Grant. (Judith Anne Still, 1996, no. 61)
Tailleferre, Germaine. (Robert Shapiro, 1994, no. 48)
Tcherepnin, Alexander. (Enrique Alberto Arias, 1989, no. 8)
Thompson, Randall. (Caroline Cepin Benser, 1991, no. 38)
Thomson, Virgil. (Michael Meckna, 1986, no. 4)
Villa-Lobos, Heitor. (David P. Appleby, 1988, no. 9)
Walton, William. (Carolyn J. Smith, 1988, no. 18)
Ward, Robert. (Kenneth Kreitner, 1988, no. 17)
Warren, Elinor Remick. (Virginia Bortin, 1993, no. 46)
Wilder, Alec. (David Demsey, 1993, no. 45)
Wuorinen, Charles. (Richard D. Burbank, 1994, no. 49)

2.55   *Composer Resource Manuals.*   Published by Garland, this series consists of bibliographic guides to information about individual composers. Each includes biographical information along with works lists, bibliography, and discography, in a selective, annotated listing. Contents of the series include the following so far (author, date of publication and volume number in parentheses):

Adam, Adolphe and Léo Delibes. (William E. Studwell, 1987, vol. 5)
Bartók, Béla. (Elliott Antokoletz, 1997, vol. 40, second edition)
Berg, Alban. (Bryan R. Simms, 1996, vol. 38)
Berlioz, Hector. (Jeffrey Alan Langford, 1989, vol. 22)
Bloch, Ernest. (David Kushner, 1988, vol. 14)
Britten, Benjamin. (Peter John Hodgson, 1996, vol. 39)
Byrd, William. (Richard Turbet, 1987, vol. 7)
Debussy, Claude. (James R. Briscoe, 1990, vol. 27)
Elgar, Edward. (Christopher Kent, 1993, vol. 37)
Falla, Manuel de. (Gilbert Chase, 1986, vol. 4)
Foster, Stephen Collins. (Calvin Elliker, 1988, vol. 10)

Frescobaldi, Girolamo. (Frederick Hammond, 1987, vol. 9)

Gluck, Christoph Willibald. (Patricia Howard,1987, vol. 8)

Handel, G. F. (Mary Ann Parker-Hale, 1988, vol. 19)

Haydn, Franz Joseph. (Floyd K. Grave, 1990, vol. 31)

Isaac, Henricus. (Martin Picker, 1991, vol. 35)

Josquin des Prez. (Charles, Sydney Robinson, 1983, vol. 2)

Kodály, Zoltán. (Philip Tacka, expected 1998, vol. 44)

Lasso, Orlando di. (James Erb, 1990, vol. 25)

Liszt, Franz. (Michael Benton Saffle, 1991, vol. 29)

Machaut, Guillaume de. (Lawrence Marshburn Earp, 1995, vol. 36)

Mahler, Gustav and Alma Mahler. (Susan Melanie Filler, 1989, vol. 28)

Monteverdi, Claudio. (K. Gary Adams, 1989, vol. 23)

Mozart, Wolfgang Amadeus. (Baird Hastings, 1989, vol. 16)

Nielsen, Carl. (Mina F. Miller, 1987, vol. 6)

Ockeghem, Johannes and Jacob Obrecht. (Martin Picker, 1988, vol. 13)

Pergolesi, Giovanni Battista. (Marvin E. Paymer, 1989, vol. 26)

Purcell, Henry. (Franklin B. Zimmerman, 1989, vol. 18)

Rachmaninoff, Sergei Vasilevich. (Robert Palmieri, 1985, vol. 3)

Rameau, Jean-Philippe. (Donald H. Foster, 1989, vol. 20)

Rimsky-Korsakov, Nikolai. (Gerald R. Seaman, 1988, vol. 17)

Scarlatti, Allessandro and Domenico Scarlatti. (Carole Franklin Vidali, 1993, vol. 34)

Schütz, Heinrich. (Allen B. Skei, 1981, vol. 1)

Sibelius, Jean. (Glenda Dawn Goss, expected 1998, vol. 41)

Vaughan Williams, Ralph. (Neil Butterworth, 1990, vol. 21)

Victoria, Tomás Luis de. (Eugene Cramer, expected 1998, vol. 43)

Vivaldi, Antonio. (Michael Talbot, 1988, vol. 12)

Weber, Carl Maria von. (Donald G. Henderson, 1990, vol. 24)

Wolf, Hugo. (David Ossenkop, 1988, vol. 15)

3

Synopses, Translations, and Diction

SYNOPSES

3.1   *Cambridge Opera Handbooks.*   Cambridge, England; New York: Cambridge University Press.

The general preface for the series states that each volume centers on three areas of concern: the historical, the analytical, and the critical. Each includes a select bibliography and discography and guides to other sources. Following is a listing of titles in the series to date, arranged alphabetically by the author:

Bauman, Thomas. *W. A. Mozart, Die Entführung aus dem Serail.* 1987.
Beckett, Lucy. *Richard Wagner, Parsifal.* 1981.
Birkin, Kenneth. *Richard Strauss, Arabella.* 1989.
Branscombe, Peter. *W. A. Mozart, Die Zauberflöte.* 1991.
Brett, Philip. *Benjamin Britten, Peter Grimes.* 1983.
Brown, Bruce Alan. *W. A. Mozart. Così fan tutte.* 1995.
Carner, Mosco. *Giacomo Puccini, Tosca.* 1985.
Carter, Tim. *W. A. Mozart, Le Nozze di Figaro.* 1987.
Cooke, Mervyn. *Benjamin Britten, Billy Budd.* 1993.
Griffiths, Paul. *Igor Stravinsky, The Rake's Progress.* 1982.
Groos, Arthur. *Giacomo Puccini, La Bohème.* 1986.
Hepokoski, James A. *Giuseppe Verdi, Falstaff.* 1983.
Hepokoski, James. *Giuseppe Verdi, Otello.* 1987.
Hinton, Stephen. *Kurt Weill, The Threepenny Opera.* 1990.
Howard, Patricia. *Benjamin Britten, The Turn of the Screw.* 1985.
Howard, Patricia. *C. W. von Gluck, Orfeo.* 1981.
Jarman, Douglas. *Alban Berg, Lulu.* 1991.
Jarman, Douglas. *Alban Berg, Wozzeck.* 1989.

Jefferson, Alan. *Richard Strauss, Der Rosenkavalier.* 1985.
Kemp, Ian. *Hector Berlioz, Les Troyens.* 1988.
McClary, Susan. *Georges Bizet, Carmen.* 1992.
Mitchell, Donald. *Benjamin Britten, Death in Venice.* 1987.
Nichols, Roger. *Claude Debussy, Pelléas et Mélisande.* 1989.
Puffett, Derrick. *Richard Strauss, Elektra.* 1989.
Puffett, Derrick. *Richard Strauss, Salome.* 1989.
Rice, John A. *W. A. Mozart, La Clemenza di Tito.* 1991.
Robinson, Paul. *Ludwig van Beethoven, Fidelio.* 1996.
Rushton, Julian. *W. A. Mozart, Don Giovanni.* 1981.
Rushton, Julian. *W. A. Mozart, Idomeneo.* 1993.
Tyrrell, John. *Leos Janacek, Kátya Kabanová.* 1982.
Warrack, John Hamilton. *Richard Wagner, Die Meistersinger von Nürnberg.* 1994.
Whenham, John. *Claudio Monteverdi, Orfeo.* 1986.

3.2   Cross, Milton. *The New Milton Cross' Complete Stories of the Great Operas.* Rev. and enl. ed. 688 pp. New York: Doubleday, 1967.

Some version of the Milton Cross books will be found in any library. Readers should also look for varying editions of *Stories of the Great Operas* (Washington Square Press, 1967), *Favorite Arias from the Great Operas* (Doubleday, 1958), and *The New Milton Cross' More Stories of the Great Operas* (Doubleday, 1980).

3.3   Drinkrow, John. *The Operetta Book.* 124 pp. New York: Drake Publishers, Inc., 1973.

Presents details on origin, plots, principal numbers and discographies of forty-nine works by twenty-one composers, all having originated in France, German or Austria.

3.4   Drone, J. M. *Index to Opera, Operetta and Musical Comedy Synopses in Collections and Periodicals.* 177 pp. Metuchen, N. J.: The Scarecrow Press, 1978.

An index to seventy-four collections and four periodical titles that includes 1,605 titles by 627 composers.

3.5   *English National Opera Guides.* Nicholas John, series editor. London:
         John Calder; New York: Riverrun Press.

The aim of the series is to prepare the opera-goer by providing the libretto in
both the original language and in English along with supplemental essays. The
current listing of titles is listed here in alphabetical order by composer:

Bartók, Béla. *The Stage Works of Béla Bartók.* 1991.
Beethoven, Ludwig van. *Fidelio.* 92 pp. 1986.
Berg, Alban. *Wozzeck.* 1990.
Bizet, Georges. *Carmen.* 1982.
Britten, Benjamin. *Peter Grimes; Gloriana.* 128 pp. 1983.
Debussy, Claude. *Pelléas & Mélisande.* 1982.
Janacek, Leos. *Jenufa; Kátya Kabanová.* 1985.
Massenet, Jules. *Manon.* 1984.
Monteverdi, Claudio. *The Operas of Monteverdi.* 1992.
Mozart, Wolfgang Amadeus. *Cosí fan tutte.* 1983.
Mozart, Wolfgang Amadeus. *Don Giovanni.* 1983.
Mozart, Wolfgang Amadeus. *Le Nozze di Figaro.* 1983.
Mozart, Wolfgang Amadeus. *The Magic Flute.* 128 pp. 1980.
Mussorgsky, Modest Petrovich. *Boris Godunov.* 112 pp. 1982.
Mussorgsky, Modest Petrovich. *Khovanshchina.* 1994.
Puccini, Giacomo. *La Bohème.* 1982.
Puccini, Giacomo. *Madama Butterfly.* 1984.
Puccini, Giacomo. *Tosca.* 1982.
Puccini, Giacomo. *Turandot.*1984.
Rossini, Gioacchino. *The Barber of Seville.* .1985.
Rossini, Gioachino. *La Cenerentola.* 96 pp. 1980.
Strauss, Richard. *Arabella.* 112 pp. 1985.
Strauss, Richard. *Der Rosenkavalier.* 128 pp. 1981.
Strauss, Richard. *Salome, Elektra.* 1988.
Stravinsky, Igor. *Oedipus Rex ; The Rake's Progress.* 1991.
Tchaikovsky, Peter Ilich. *Eugene Onegin.* 1988.
Tippett, Michael. *The Operas of Michael Tippet.* 144 pp. 1985.
Verdi, Giuseppe. *Aida.* 96 pp. 1980.
Verdi, Giuseppe. *Don Carlos.* 1992.
Verdi, Giuseppe. *Falstaff.* 1982.
Verdi, Giuseppe. *Il Trovatore.* 1983.
Verdi, Giuseppe. *La Traviata.* 80 pp. 1981.
Verdi, Giuseppe. *Macbeth.* 1990.
Verdi, Giuseppe. *Otello.* 80 pp. 1988.
Verdi, Giuseppe. *Rigoletto.* 1982.

Verdi, Giuseppe. *Simon Boccanegra*. 96 pp. 1985.
Verdi, Giuseppe. *Un Ballo in Maschera*. 1989.
Wagner, Richard. *Der Fliegende Holländer*. 1982.
Wagner, Richard. *Die Meistersinger von Nürnberg*. 1983.
Wagner, Richard. *Lohengrin*. 1993.
Wagner, Richard. *Siegfried*. 1984.
Wagner, Richard. *Tannhäuser*. 1988.
Wagner, Richard. *The Rheingold*. 1985.
Wagner, Richard. *Tristan and Isolde*. Revised edition. 96 pp. 1983.
Wagner, Richard. *Twilight of the Gods: Götterdammerung*. 1985.

3.6   Ewen, David. *The Book of European Light Opera*. 297 pp. Westport,
        Conn.: Greenwood Press, 1977.

Originally published in 1962 by Holt, Rinehard and Winston (New York). The
subtitle of the book describes it best: "A guide to 167 European comic operas,
light operas, operettas, opéra-comiques, opéra-bouffes, and opera buffas from *The
Beggar's Opera* (1728) and *La Serva Padrona* (1733) to Ivor Novello's *King's
Rhapsody* (1949), by eighty-one composers, with plot, production history,
musical highlights, critical evaluations, and other relevant information."

3.7   Forman, Denis. *A Night at the Opera: An Irreverent Guide to the
        Plots, the Singers, the Composers, the Recordings*. 1st U. S. edition.
        959 pp. New York: Random House, 1995.

A humorous look at seventeen of the most popular operas. Fun to read.
Originally published as *The Good Opera Guide* in 1994 by Weidenfeld &
Nicolson (London).

3.8   Freeman, John W. *Metropolitan Opera Stories of the Great Operas*. 2
        vols. New York: Metropolitan Opera Guild, 1984-1997.

Brief synopses of well over 250 operas between the two volumes. Another
book, written by Jack Sacher, *Opera: A Listener's Guide* (Schirmer Books,
1997, examines eleven operas in detail. Sacher has been a lecturer on opera for
the Metropolitan Opera Guild since 1964.

3.9   Gänzl, Kurt and Andrew Lamb. *Gänzl's Book of the Musical Theatre.*
         1,353 pp. New York: Schirmer Books, 1989.

First published by Bodley Head (London, 1988). Cleverly written synopses of
some 300 musical theater productions. Divided by nationality, with helpful
introductory essays at the beginning of each section. Indexes to song titles as
well as to production personnel enhance the volume's usefulness, as does a
healthy discography.

3.10   Hardwick, Michael. *The Drake Guide to Gilbert and Sullivan.* 284 pp.
         New York: Drake Publishers Inc., 1973.

Previously published in 1972 (Osprey, Reading). A handy guide to the works
and the characters created by Gilbert and Sullivan. Includes an index of first
lines, a "Gilbertian Glossary" which clarifies much of the text which is
unfamiliar in the present day, especially to non-British singers and audiences, a
discography and a selective bibliography.

3.11   Harewood, George Lascelles, Earl of. *The New Kobbe's Opera Book.*
         1,012 pp. New York: Putnam, 1997.

Revised edition of *The Definitive Kobbe's Opera Book.* This is the most recent
version of the Kobbe, which is a collection of synopses. Other versions include
The Pocket Kobbe's Opera Book (Bodley Head, 1994), *The Portable Kobbe's
Opera Guide* (Berkley, 1994), *Kobbe's Illustrated Opera Book: Thirty-two of the
World's Best-loved Operas.* (Bodley Head, 1991), as well as the previously
published edition, *Kobbe's Illustrated Opera Book: Twenty-six of the World's
Best-loved Operas* (1989), and finally the 10th edition of *Kobbe's Complete
Opera Book* (Bodley Head, 1987, 1st American ed. published in the same year by
Putnam).

3.12   Jacobs, Arthur, and Stanley Sadie. *The Pan Book of Opera.* Enlarged
         edition. 563 pp. London: Pan Books, 1984.

First published in 1964. A guide to eighty-three operas by forty-one composers
from Monteverdi to Berg. See also the American edition, *Opera: a Modern
Guide* by the same authors (New York: Drake, 1972) which covers sixty-three
operas by thirty-two composers.

3.13   *Lyric Opera Companion: The History, Lore, and Stories of the World's Greatest Operas.* 449 pp. Kansas City, Mo.: Andrews and McMeel, 1991.

Entertaining essays on eighty-eight operas, written by several writers that offer different information from the standard opera synopses collections.

3.14   Martin, George. *The Companion to Twentieth-century Opera.* 653 pp. New York: Dodd, Mead & Company, 1979.

Divided into three parts: Part I is a group of seven essays on modern opera; Part II offers synopses of seventy-eight operas by twenty-two composers, including information on timings for scenes, usual cuts, related offstage events, vocabulary listings of key words and phrases; and Part III, which includes pertinent facts and figures on the performance activities of twenty-three leading opera companies.

3.15   Martin, George. *The Opera Companion.* 693 pp. New York: Dodd, Mead & Company, 1982.

Divided into three parts: "The Casual Operagoer's Guide," "Glossary" and "The Synopses." It is the author's goal to provide the reader with ample information to become an informed opera-goer. Part I provides background information on everything from voice and orchestration to ballet and claques. The glossary offers definitions of operatic terms and related miscellanea, e.g. 'alfresco' and 'aria,' 'barbershop' and 'brindisi,' 'patter song' and 'Patti.' The synopses portion covers forty-seven operas, in uncut versions, indicating where cuts are sometimes taken. Also includes average timings of the acts, and vocabulary lists of words audience members *should* more than likely hear during performance. There are two appendixes; one listing the operas mentioned in the book and one on basic operatic Italian.

3.16   Studwell, William E. and David A. Hamilton. *Opera Plot Index: A Guide to Locating Plots and Descriptions of Operas, Operettas, and Other Works of Musical Theater and Associated Material.* 446 pp. New York: Garland, 1990.

Indexes information on approximately 2900 works found in 169 sources. Arranged alphabetically by title. There is an index to composers.

TRANSLATIONS

3.17   Castel, Nico.   *The Complete Puccini Libretti.*   Geneseo, N.Y.:
        Leyerle, 1993 - .

IPA transcriptions and word-for-word translations including a guide to the IPA.

3.18   Castel, Nico. *The Complete Verdi Libretti.* 4 vols. Geneseo, N.Y.:
        Leyerle, 1994.

IPA transcriptions and word-for-word translations including a guide to the IPA.

3.19   Castel, Nico. *The Libretti of Mozart's Completed Operas.* 2 vols.
        Geneseo, N. Y.: Leyerle, 1997 - .

IPA transcriptions and word-for-word translations including a guide to the IPA.

3.20   Cobb, Margaret. *The Poetic Debussy: A Collection of His Song Texts
        and Selected Letters.* 2nd ed. 326 pp. Rochester, N.Y.: University of
        Rochester, 1994.

Translations by Richard Miller. Translations and notes for all ninety-two songs,
including those that were never completed or published. Also included are letters
written between 1889 and 1917, which shed light on Debussy's knowledge of
poetry. Indexes of both titles and first lines. Bibliography.

3.21   Cockburn, Jacqueline, and Richard Stokes.   *The Spanish Song
        Companion.* 268 pp. London: Victor Gollancz, Ltd., 1992.

Not only translations, but something of an historical overview of Spanish song,
starting with monody, moving though the *tonadilla* and *zarzuela* through the
present day. Appendix includes translations of texts by Spanish poets set by
Brahms, Wolf, and Schumann. Indexes of composers, poets, translations, titles
and first lines.

3.22   Coffin, Berton, Werner Singer, and Pierre Delattre. *Word-by-word Translations of Songs and Arias. Part I: German and French.* 260 pp. New York: The Scarecrow Press, 1966.
Schoep, Arthur, and Daniel Harris. *Word-by-word Translations of Songs and Arias. Part II: Italian.* 563 pp. Methuchen, N. J.: The Scarecrow Press, Inc., 1972.

Affectionately known as "the grey books" by many music librarians, voice teachers and singers. Arranged alphabetically by composer, the translations are word-for-word, with a more poetic version added paranthetically when deemed necessary by the compilers. No IPA in these volumes because those are contained in Coffin's *Phonetic Readings of Songs and Arias* (3.43) . Written to accompany Coffin's *The Singer's Repertoire* (2nd ed., Scarecrow, 1960), which is a classified listing of solo vocal repertoire. There are separate volumes for lyric and dramatic soprano, mezzo and contralto, lyric and dramatic tenor, and baritone and bass. There is an additional volume containg program notes.

3.23   Fischer-Dieskau, Dietrich. *The Fischer-Dieskau Book of Lieder: The Original Texts of Over Seven Hundred and Fifty Songs.* With English translations by George Bird and Richard Stokes. 437 pp. New York: Alfred A. Knopf, 1977.

Initially published in German as *Texte deutscher Lieder* in 1976. Limelight Editions published a paperback ed. in 1984 and another in 1995. There is an essay on artsong by Fischer-Dieskau. The texts are arranged by the German title and an English translation is presented on the facing page. Included with each poem are the poet's name and a list of musical settings. There are indexes for composer, poet and translator, and title and first line.

3.24   Glass, Beaumont. *Schubert's Complete Song Texts.* Vol. 1 - . Geneseo, N. Y.: Leyerle, 1996- .

IPA transcriptions with word-for-word translations.

3.25   Goldovsky, Boris and Arthur Schoep. *Bringing Soprano Arias to Life.* 320 pp. Metuchen, N. J.: The Scarecrow Press, 1991.

Reprint of 1973 G. Schirmer edition. Careful examination of twenty-eight of the most commonly heard operatic arias from the standard repertoire for sopranos, providing the singer with information on the drama, musical aspects and, more specifically, vocal aspects and possibly problematic phrases. Also includes both literal and idiomatic translations of the text and staging suggestions, along with a drawing of the particular character and costume for each aria. No index.

3.26   Jeffers, Ron. *Translations and Annotations of Choral Repertoire*. Vol. 1, *Sacred Latin Texts*. Corvallis, Ore.: Earthsongs, 1988.

A most helpful volume for locating translations and explanations of sacred texts, such as the Roman and Requiem Masses and others. Information is also included for the liturgical year and the Divine Office. Includes both Roman and Austro-German pronunciation guides.

3.27   Larrick, Geary. *Musical References and Song Texts in the Bible*. 152 pp. Lewiston, N. Y.: The Edwin Mellen Press, 1990.

The first section cites the many musical reference in the Bible, but it is the second section that is valuable to singers. Here readers will find scriptural citations and English texts to the Magnificat and The Song of Solomon, among others.

3.28   Le Van, Timothy. *Masters of Italian Art Songs; Word-by-word and Poetic Translations of the Complete Songs for Voice and Piano*. 321 pp. Metuchen, N. J.: The Scarecrow Press, Inc., 1990.

Le Van, an accompanist/coach, offers translations for the complete songs by Bellini, Donaudy, Donizetti, Puccini, Rossini, Tosti and Verdi. He uses a three-line format: Italian text; word-by-word; poetic translations. Title and first line indexes.

3.29   Le Van, Timothy. *Masters of the French Art Song: Translations of the Complete Songs for Voice and Piano*. 445 pp. Methuchen, N. J.: The Scarecrow Press, Inc., 1991.

Follows the same format as 3.28, covering the songs of Chausson, Debussy, Duparc, Fauré and Ravel.

3.30   Miller, Philip L. *German Lieder.* 336 pp. New York: Continuum, 1990. (The German library, 42)

Offers English translations of texts to the poetry. Arranged by composer. Indexes to composers, poets, and titles and first lines.

3.31   Miller, Philip L. *The Ring of Words: An Anthology of Song Texts.* 518 pp. New York: Norton, 1973.

Originally published in 1963 by Doubleday, New York. "Bright is the ring of words when the right man rings them, Fair the fall of songs when the singer sings them" begins the poem by Robert Louis Stevenson. This anthology of song texts in translation is aptly named as it includes over 300 songs from seven countries, accompanied by line-by-line translations into English. The compiler begins the anthology with an essay on the art song. The texts are arranged first by country and then alphabetically by poet. There are indexes for composers and titles/first lines.

3.32   Phillips, Lois. *Lieder Line by Line and Word for Word.* Revised ed. 434 pp. Oxford: Clarendon Press, 1996.

Translations of poems set by Beethoven, Schubert, Schumann, Wagner, Brahms, Wolf, Mahler and Strauss. Includes prose versions of the poems, but no IPA. Combined title/first line index.

3.33   Rachmaninoff, Sergei. *The Singer's Rachmaninoff* . Edited with introduction and translations by Natalia Challis. 258 pp. New York: Pelion Press, 1989.

The first chapter covers Russian diction and pronunciation, including the Russian alphabet and related IPA symbols, along with a short bibliography at the end of the chapter. Chapters 2 and 3 provide background on the composer, Russia and the country's poetical tradition. The remaining chapters cover the songs, background information, both literal and syntactical translations, and IPA transcription. There is a useful chronology in the Appendix, as well as numerous indexes.

3.34   Reed, John. *The Schubert Song Companion.* 510 pp. Manchester, England: Manchester University Press, 1985.

A comprehensive guide to the songs, in alphabetical order by title. Each entry includes the incipit, a translation of the text, and accompanying notes. Part II is a biographical dictionary of sorts for the authors. There are appendixes that range in topics from the tonalities of the songs to publication information to tempo indications and markings.

3.35   Richardson, Dorothy, and Tina Ruta. *Arie Antiche.* 147 pp. Orleans, Mass.: Paraclete Press, 1990.

Accompanies the Ricordi edition of Parisotti's arias and songs (Milan, 1885-1990, 3 vols.) Includes both literal and poetic translations. Indexes lead the user to the appropriate Ricordi volume by either composer or title.

3.36   Rohinsky, Marie-Claire. *The Singer's Debussy.* 317 pp. New York: Pelion Press, 1987.

Chapters on pronunciation and diction, along with a listing of the songs, complete with IPA symbols, word-by-word translations and poetical translations. Indexed by titles and first lines.

3.37   Schumann, Robert. *The Singer's Schumann.* Edited with introduction and translations by Thilo Reinhard. 423 pp. New York: Pelion Press, 1988.

Compiled by an accompanist for singers, this volume includes essays on Schumann and the lied, the poets, German pronunciation and diction, transposition and key character. There is also a translation of portions of Schumann's "Musical Rules for Home and Life." Included are literal and poetical translations, along with the IPA transcriptions and background information. A chronology "Robert Schumann and his time," indexes of songs by opus number, title/first line indexes, a bibliography, a works list and a general index complete the volume.

3.38   Sobrer, Josep Miquel and Edmon Colomer. *The Singer's Anthology of 20th Century Spanish Songs.* 203 pp. New York: Pelion Press, 1987.

Provides translations, both literal and syntactical, and IPA transcriptions for songs by Granados, Falla, and Mompou. The first chapter covers diction and interpretation of IPA symbols in both Spanish and Catalan. Topics covered by four appendixes are biographical information of the composers; lists of published songs; index of song titles and of first lines.

3.39   Unger, Melvin P. *Handbook to Bach's Sacred Cantata Texts: An Interlinear Translation with Reference Guide to Biblical Quotations and Illusions.* 776 pp. Metuchen, N. J.: The Scarecrow Press, 1996.

Arranged by BWV number, the text is presented in German, with the English translation running along underneath. The scriptural quotation is in the facing column. Included are reference numbers for the *Neue Bach Ausgabe* and the *Bach Compendium*. Nine indexes provide access to the information in the body of the text. There is also a selected bibliography.

3.40   Wigmore, Richard. *Schubert: The Complete Song Texts.* 380 pp. London: Victor Gollancz, Ltd., 1988.

The first book to collect the texts and prose translations for all of Schubert's surviving completed solo songs for voice and piano; also including others such as *Auf dem Strom* and *Der Hirt auf dem Felsen.* Arranged alphabetically by titles, with poet, Deutsch number and year of composition. Includes index of first lines.

DICTION

3.41   Alton, Jeannine, and Brian Jeffery. *Bele Buche e Bele Parleure: A Guide to Pronunciation of Medieval and Renaissance French for Singers and Others.* 80 pp. + cassette. London: Tecla; San Francisco: Pacific Coast Music, 1976.

A guide to pronunciation, including regional dialects. Includes twelve poems on the accompanying cassette, all spoken, and six of them presented in musical settings.

3.42   Castel, Nico. *A Singer's Manual of Spanish Lyric Diction.* 162 pp. New York: Excalibur Pub., 1994.

A thorough explanation of every aspect of Spanish diction, including a chapter on Ladino, the language of the Spanish Sephardic Jews.

3.43   Coffin, Berton, Pierre Delattre, Ralph Errole, and Werner Singer. *Phonetic Readings of Songs and Arias.* 361 pp. Reprint. Metuchen, N. J. and London: The Scarecrow Press, 1981.

First published in 1963 by Pruett Press (Boulder, Colo.) This companion volume to *The Singer's Repertoire* offers IPA transcriptions of the repertoire included therein.

3.44   Colorni, Evelina. *Singers' Italian: A Manual of Diction and Phonetics.* 150 pp. New York: Schirmer, 1970.

The author concentrates on aspects of lyric diction. Included along with the standard chapters on pronunciation are chapters on syllabication and pronouncing words in context, taking into consideration the predominance of vowels and their lengths, the number of vowels sometimes occurring in one note, contiguous consonants, and so on. There is a bibliography.

3.45   Copeman, Harold. 359 pp. *Singing in Latin; or Pronunciation Explor'd.* Oxford: 22 Tawney St., The Author, 1990.

A scholarly guide to pronunciation of Latin texts "with some semblance of historical and stylistic respectability" to quote the author. The preface is written by Andrew Parrott. The author's *The Pocket Singing in Latin* should also be noted.

3.46   Cox, Richard G. *The Singer's Manual of German and French Diction.* 63 pp. New York: Schirmer, 1970.

Straightforward outline of the pronunciation of German and French for the beginner. The author also includes appendixes which cover common German prefixes and prepositions used as prefixes, exercises in "adjacent" French vowel sounds, and sample transcriptions of both German and French texts. Brief bibliography. No index.

3.47   Cox, Richard. *Singing in English: A Manual of English Diction for Singers and Choral Directors.* 109 pp. Lawton, Okla.: ACDA, 1990.

Although it is written with choral singers in mind, any singer will benefit from reading this book. It covers all the basics, with the underlying emphasis that "Good diction ought to facilitate good vocal technique, since both are dependent on free and flexible activity of jaw, tongue, and lips." (p. 1)

3.48   Donnan, Thomas M. *French Lyric Diction.* 144 pp. Lanham, MD: University Press of America, 1994.

3.49   Farish, Stephen. *French Diction for Singers.* 142 pp. Denton, TX: Gore Pub., 1994.

A manual on singing in French written by a voice teacher.

3.50   Forward, Geoffrey G. *American Diction for Singers.* 464 pp. + two cassettes. Los Angeles, Calif.: Vocal Power Institute, 1990.

This "self-help" text and workbook on diction will introduce the reader to a thorough examination of the various components of good diction. It also provides background on American English and its various dialects, as well as Standard American Stage Dialect. Along with the chapters on basic diction, there is a chapter on "pop pronunciation."

3.51   Grubb, Thomas. *Singing in French; A Manual of French Diction and French Vocal Repertoire.* 221 pp. + sound recording. New York: Schirmer Books; London: Collier Macmillan Publishers, 1979.

Written to be used either as a textbook for the diction classroom or in the studio, covers standard areas such as "singing the sounds" of French, liaison, phoneticization and preparation of a song or aria, application of diction techniques to other aspects of singing, and a fairly comprehensive repertoire list. Appendixes provide lists of vowels and consonants, either single or in combination, and the proper pronunciation in any given circumstance, along with examples. There is also a listing entitled "Pronunciation of Proper Nouns Pertaining to the Repertoire," a bibliography, and an answer key to the exercises included in the text.

3.52   Hines, Robert S. *Singer's Manual of Latin Diction and Phonetics.* 86
        pp.   New York: Schirmer Books; London: Collier Macmillan
        Publishers, 1975.

A great deal of information in a very few pages. Includes an essay on Liturgical
Latin, glossary of terms used in phonetics, and thorough discussions of Latin
vowels and consonants. Also includes translations for the numerous Latin texts
which all singers, whether soloist or chorister, perform throughout their careers.

3.53   Magner, Candace A. *Phonetic Readings of Brahms Lieder.* 412 pp.
        Metuchen, N.J.: The Scarecrow Press, 1987.

Offers all of Brahms's songs in IPA with the German text included above, line
by line. Appendixes lead the user to the appropriate text through indexes listed
by opus number, title, first line, or poet. There is a title/first line index as well.

3.54   Magner, Candace A. *Phonetic Readings of Schubert's Lieder.* 2 vols.
        Metuchen, N. J.: The Scarecrow Press, 1994.

Following the same format as its partner volume on Brahms songs, provides
IPA and German texts for all Schubert lieder, line by line.

3.55   Marshall, Yale. *Singing Fluent American Vowels.* 258 pp.   Rev.
        version. Minneapolis, Minn.: Pro Musica, 1994.

The author, a tenor and vocal coach, presents his theories about American
English and singing. Of special note is the portion of the book that traces the
development of American English.

3.56   McGee, Timothy, A. G. Rigg, and David N. Klausner. *Singing Early
        Music: The Pronunciation of European Languages in the Late Midde
        Ages and Renaissance.* 299 pp. + compact disc. Bloomington: Indiana
        University Press, 1996. (Music: Scholarship and Performance)

Twelve contributing authors offer guides to pronunciation of languages from
Britain, France, the Iberian Peninsula, Italy, and Germany and the Low
Countries. Recorded examples for each chapter are found on the accompanying
CD.   There is a glossary of language-related terms (e.g. africate, disyllablic,

prepalatal, etc.), a contents list for the CD, and an IPA-based phonetics chart. No index.

3.57   Moriarty, John. *Diction: Italian, Latin, French, German...the Sounds and 81 Exercises for Singing Them.* 263 pp. Boston: E.C. Schirmer Music Company, 1975.

The author first devised this text for his diction classes for the apprentice program at the Santa Fe Opera and then for with his students at the New England Conservatory. Includes bibliography and index of sounds.

3.58   Odom, William. *German for Singers; A Textbook of Diction and Phonetics.* 169 pp. New York: Schirmer Books; London: Collier Macmillan Publishers, 1981.

The two purposes of the book are to provide a systematic approach to German pronunciation and to provide a shorthand for singers to use as guideposts in their singing. Designed as a textbook for university-level diction courses. Divided into two parts: "Phonetics" and "The Sounds Of German." Includes an alphabetic index that provides the reader with a thorough listing of the alphabetic combinations, pronunciation, positions, examples and pages in the text that treat them. Exercises are included at the end of the chapters.

3.59   Piatak, Jean and Regina Avrashov. *Russian Songs & Arias; Phonetic Readings, Word-by-Word Translations; and a Concise Guide to Russian Diction.* 206 pp. Dallas, Tex.: Pst...Inc., 1991.

Consists of two parts: Russian diction and phonetic readings and translations of selected Russian operatic arias and songs. There is a basic bibliography and there are title/first line indexes for both Russian and English.

3.60   Thomson, Robert S. *Italian for the Opera.* 160 pp. Vancouver: The Author (P. O. Box 4781, Vancouver, B. C., V6B 4R4), 1992.

The author outlines the differences between spoken Italian and operatic Italian.

3.61   Uris, Dorothy. *To Sing in English: A Guide to Improved Diction.* 317 pp. New York; London: Boosey and Hawkes, 1971.

The author, who was an instructor in diction and speech at the Mannes College of Music and the Manhattan School of Music, discusses the various components required to sing in English by examining everything from "The importance of unimportant word" to the legato qualities of the English language to the vowel content of American English.   Appendixes include a discussion on dialects, suggested recordings and bibliography. There is an index.

3.62   Wall, Joan. *Diction for Singers: a Concise Reference for English, Italian, Latin, German, French and Spanish Pronunciation.* 279 pp. Dallas, Tex.: Pst...Inc., 1990.

Intended for use as a textbook for undergraduate diction classes, each chapter is divided into three sections: charts describing the sounds of letters in a particular language, the general rules of pronunciation, and a detailed description of each vowel and consonant, as well as groupings of letters unique to that language. The chapter on Latin diction includes the Ordinary of the Mass, transcribed into IPA, and a translation.

3.63   Wall, Joan. *International Phonetic Alphabet for Singers.* 226 pp. Dallas, TX: Pst..., Inc., 1988.

Both a textbook and a workbook for any singer who needs a thorough grounding in the use of the International Phonetic Alphabet. Includes drawings and precise positions for tongue, jaw, lips and soft palate, along with common problems associated with the pronunciation of the particular sound. There are copious exercises throughout the text, including transcriptions of words into IPA, and an answer key.

3.64   Wierenga, L. *French Diction for the Singer: A Phonetics Workbook.* 64 pp. Kenyon Pub, 1977.

The study of pronunciation of French for singers, outlined in six chapters which are devoted to oral vowels; nasal vowels; semi-vowels; consonants; syllables, stress, and liaison; and the application of phonetics to singing.

4

Preparation, Accompanying, Coaching

4.1   Bernac, Pierre. *The Interpretation of French Song.* 2nd ed. 327 pp. London: Gollancz, 1976.

First published by Praeger in 1970; also published by Cassell in London. Includes chapters that discuss interpretation and performance of French song literature. Includes texts and translations of songs by sixteen composers, among them Berlioz, Bizet, Chabrier, Debussy, Duparc, Franck, Poulenc, Ravel and Satie. There are lists of additional composers and their songs. Indexes for titles, first lines, and composers.

4.2   Caldwell, Robert. *The Performer Prepares.* 158 pp. Dallas, Tex.: Pst...Inc., 1990.

Working from the premise that successful performance skills can be learned, the author offers an approach for the preparation of a confident performer. Topics covered include "Imagining the Performance," "Artistic Grit," "Stage Fright," and "Connecting with the Audience."

4.3   Dunsby, Jonathan. *Performing Music: Shared Concerns.* 112 pp. Oxford: Clarendon Press, 1995.

The author, himself a pianist and professor of music, explores the various aspects of musical performance. Written from the pianist's standpoint, there is still considerable information for the singing performer -- or any performer, for that matter. Bibliography included.

4.4   Emmons, Shirlee and Stanley Sonntag. *The Art of the Song Recital.* 571 pp. New York: Schirmer Books, 1979.

Designed to provide both singer and accompanist with succinct and useful information for creating successful recitals. Includes a chapter on the history of the song recital, several chapters on the techniques of program building for all levels of singers, chapters that survey various types of vocal music including contemporary music, chamber music, song cycles, folk and popular music. Almost half of the book includes an Appendix that provides several repertoire lists and a publisher's list, which, though somewhat out of date, includes addresses and American agents where applicable, some of which may still be correct. Bibliography, no index.

4.5   Gorrell, Lorraine. *The Nineteenth-Century German Lied.*   398 pp. Portland, Ore.: Amadeus Press, 1993.

Examines the songs of Beethoven, Schubert, Schumann, Fanny Hensel, Mendelssohn, Liszt, Wagner, Brahms, Wolf, Mahler and Strauss, as well as topics that include poetry and music, politics and poetry, and women musicians of the day. Three appendices include a chronology, a listing of performing editions of songs by lesser-known composers, and a section on program planning. There is a bibliography, song indexes by both title and composer, and a subject index.

4.6   Grindea, Caroloa. *Tensions in the Performance of Music.* Revised and enlarged ed. 204 pp. London: Kahn & Averill, 1995.

A collection of essays that address tension and performance issues for all musicians. Some are dedicated specifically to the voice, but there is something to be learned from reading all of them.

4.7   Hallmark, Rufus. *German Lieder in the Nineteenth Century* 346 pp.
         New York: Schirmer Books, 1996. (Studies in Musical Genres and
         Repertories)

A collection of essays by noted scholars which include topics such as "The
Literary Context: Goethe as Source and Catalyst" by Harry Seelig; "Franz
Schubert: The Prince of Song" by Susan Youens; "Robert Schumann: The Poet
Sings" by Rufus Hallmark. Other essays include Virginia Hancock's "Johannes
Brahms: Volkslied/Kunstlied," Jurgen Thym's "Crosscurrents in Song: Five
Distinctive Voices," Lawrence Kramer's "Hugo Wolf: Subjectivity in the Fin-de-
Siecle Lied," Christopher Lewis's "Gustav Mahler: Romantic Culmination,"
and Barbara A. Petersen's "Richard Strauss: A Lifetime of Lied Composition."
Rounding out the volume are essays by John Daverio and Robert Spillman
entitled "The Song Cycle: Journeys Through a Romantic Landscape" and
"Performing Lieder: The Mysterious Mix."

4.8   Hines, Jerome. *Great Singers on Great Singing*. 8th Limelight ed.
         356 pp. New York: Limelight, 1995.

Originally published in 1982. The great American *basso* interviews other
famous singers.

4.9   Kravitt, Edward F. *The Lied : Mirror of Late Romanticism*. 323 pp.
         New Haven, Conn.: Yale University Press, 1996.

The study shows how this musical form reflecyed the changes taking place in
society and surveys the works of five important composers: Wolf, Mahler,
Strauss, Pfitzner, and Reger. Other composers included in the discussion are
Haas, Humperdinck and Schoenberg. There is a glossary, a selective
bibliography, and an index.

4.10   Lehmann, Lotte. *Eighteen Song Cycles: Studies in Their
         Interpretation*. 185 pp. New York: Praeger Publishers, 1972.

Provides Lehmann's interpretive ideas and suggestions for those standard song
cycles composed by Beethoven, Schubert, Schumann, Brahms, Wagner, Wolf,
Mahler, R. Strauss, Berlioz, Ravel and Debussy. Includes an introductory essay
admonishing singers: "Do not build up your songs as if they were encased in
stone walls." Also includes an index of first lines and titles, but no translations.

The author explains that none were added because "the singer who wishes to study Lieder and Chansons must do so in the original language."

4.11   Lehmann, Lotte. *More than Singing; The Interpretation of Songs.* 192 pp. New York: Boosey & Hawkes, Inc., 1945. Reprint, Dover Publications, Inc., 1985.

Suggestions on interpretation of a substantial sampling of vocal literature, mostly German. Readers will note some duplication of material, although slightly reworded in places, from Lehmann's *Eighteen song Cycles.* There is no index.

4.12   Matheopoulos, Helena. *Bravo: Today's Great Tenors, Baritones and Basses Discuss Their Roles.* 338 pp. London: Weidenfeld and Nicolson, 1986.

Twenty-two opera singers discuss their methods of interpretation for the operatic roles they create. Prefatory matter includes a short glossary of musical terms and an introductory essay entitled "Opera Today". Bibliography, index, photographs.

4.13   Matheopoulos, Helena. *Diva: Great Sopranos and Mezzos Discuss Their Art.* 333 pp. Boston, Mass.; Northeastern University Press, 1992.

Interviews with twenty-six of the world's leading women of the operatic stage. Other books by this author include *Divo : Great Tenors, Baritones and Basses Discuss Their Roles; Maestro: Encounters with Conductors of Today;* and *Placido Domingo : My Roles in Opera* (expected in 1999).

4.14   Ristad, Eloise. *A Soprano on her Head.* 201 pp. Moab, Ut.: Real People Press 1982.

A book about overcoming performance anxieties.

4.15   Schneider, Sara K. *Concert Song as Seen: Kinesthetic Aspects of Musical Interpretation.* 90 pp. Stuyvesant, N.Y.: Pendragon Press, 1994.

The author discusses the effect of the "physical performance" on interpretation.

4.16   Singher, Martial. *An Interpretive Guide to Operatic Arias: A Handbook for Singers, Coaches, Teachers and Students.* 350 pp. University Park, Pa.: The Pennsylvania State University Press, 1983.

Covers 151 arias from sixty-six operas for all voice types. Singher provides thumbnail sketches that illuminate the character, the action, the background, along with a translation of the text. Written by an opera singer/teacher of over fifty years, the reader is given strong insights into the character and the aria at hand.

4.17   Stein, Deborah and Robert Spillman. *Poetry into Song; Performance and Analysis of Lieder.* 413 pp. New York; Oxford: Oxford University Press, 1996.

Foreword by Elly Ameling. Written for both the singer and the pianist, the authors examine the poetry, performance, and analysis of the music of the German Lied. Each aspect is treated individually in great detail. There is also an examination of different settings of the same poem. Performers will receive a refresher course in the basics of poetry, such as rhetorical devices and meter, along with perhaps more familiar musical aspects of interpretation. There are several appendices, including a useful glossary and a bibliography.

Performance Practice

4.18   Brown, Howard Mayer, and Stanley Sadie. *Performance Practice.* 2 vols. Basingstoke, England: Macmillan; New York and London: W. W. Norton, 1990. (New Grove Handbooks in Music) (The Norton/Grove handbooks in music)

Vol. I: Music before 1600; Vol. II: Music after 1600. This is a general overview of the topic, with information on all instruments and voices, as well as on tuning, cadenzas, etc.

4.19   Donington, Robert. *The Interpretation of Early Music.* Newly revised ed. 766 p. New York, London: W. W. Norton, 1989.

A comprehensive examination of the topic, worthy of study from cover to cover. Sections devoted specifically to the voice include "Authenticity in Early Opera," and a chapter on "The Voice." Throughout the text are discussions on ornamentation, embellishment, tremolo, vibrato, and trills, to name a few. There is an extended section on accompaniment. Equally comprehensive appendices and index round out the volume, which ends by the author's enlightening comments about the state of early music in his conclusion, "The only conclusion I wish to draw at the moment is that I have no conclusion I wish to draw. The interpretation of early music is so obviously a continuing experiment." (p. 592) Readers might also want to consult Donington's *Baroque Music: Style and Performance; A Handbook*, also published by Norton (1982).

4.20   Le Huray, Peter. *Authenticity in Performance*. 202 pp. Cambridge: Cambridge University Press, 1990.

The author choses to "define some of the more important questions that the performer and listener should ask" (p. xv) when considering authentic performance by offering a series of case studies of selected works. Of particular interest will be the chapter on Handel's *Messiah*. Not only does this chapter cover various performance aspects of the oratorio itelf, but readers can also learn a great deal about Pier Francesco Tosi's *Observations on the Florid Song...* and Bacilly's *Remarques curieuses sur l'art de bien chanter.*

4.21   Leppard, Raymond. *Authenticity in Music*. 80 pp. London: Faber Music, 1988.

Looks at the art of the recital in both historical context and as it is being taught today. Includes case studies of present-day performers. Bibliography.

4.22   Toft, Robert. *Tune Thy Musicke to Thy Hart: The Art of Eloquent Singing in England 1597-1622*. 194 pp. Toronto: University of Toronto, 1993.

The author, himself an accompanist, examines historical documents in an effort to recreate the performance practices employed in England between 1597 and 1622, which are the beginning and ending dates for the publication of books of lute-songs. The study examines both *elocutio* and *pronunciatio*, which the author maintains, are at the core of proper study and performance of this genre. In the third part of the book, the author applies these principles to the lute-songs of John Dowland for the modern singer. There is a useful glossary along with a bibliography of both primary and secondary source materials.

Oratorio

4.23   Brown, A. Peter. *Performing Haydn's The Creation: Recontructing the Earliest Renditions.* 125 pp. Bloomington: Indiana University Press, 1986. (Music -- Scholarship and performance)

A scholarly examination of the versions of the work used by Haydn himself. Most useful to singers is the chapter on embellishment and ornamentation.

4.24   Rilling, Helmuth. *Johann Sebastian Bach's B-minor Mass.* Translated by Gordon Paine, Foreword by Howard S. Swan. 154 pp. Princeton, N. J.: Prestige Publications, Inc., 1984.

Maestro Rilling is one of the leading interpreters of Bach's choral music. Moving through each movement, he analyzes Bach's intentions for the music and the reasoning behind the composer's choice of voice and instrumentation. A good resource for the soloists as well as the conductor.

4.25   Shaw, Watkins. *A Textual and Historical Companion to Handel's Messiah.* Revised edition. 213 pp. Sevenoaks: Novello, 1982.

First published in 1965. Written as a companion to the author's own edition of the oratorio, it is useful for any edition. Another useful resource is Peter Wishart's *Messiah Ornamented* (Stainer & Bell, 1974.)

4.26   Van Camp, Leonard. *A Practical Guide for Performing, Teaching and Singing Messiah.* 223 pp. Dayton, Oh.: Lorenz, 1993.

In the author's words, this is a "nuts and bolts" look at how to perform the oratorio. It includes a chapter on myths related to it, questions relating to performance which includes the various editions available, personnel required, and so forth. The bulk of the text is a movement to movement interpretive analysis. The book ends with a selected bibliography and numerous appendixes that could be useful.

Accompanying and Coaching

4.27   Adler, Kurt. *The Art of Accompanying and Coaching.* 260 pp. New York: Capo, 1980.

Reprint of the edition published by the University of Minnesota in 1965. The first book to be written on accompanying in well over one hundred years, Adler's text is meant to "be an aid to pianists who want to become or already are professional accompanists or coaches." (p. 5) In eleven chapters, the author explores the history of both accompanying and coaching, musical instruments, phonetics and diction, style, program-building, and the art of both accompanying and coaching. Useful bibliography and thorough index.

4.28   Cranmer, Philip. *The Technique of Accompaniment.* 108 pp. London: Dobson, 1970.

Thirteen chapters that deal with all aspects of being an accompanist, including rehearsals, sight-reading, and transposition. Equally useful to the beginning student of accompanying as to the professional.

4.29   Moore, Gerald. *The Unashamed Accompanist.* Rev. ed. 126 pp. London: Julia MacRae Books, 1984.

First published in 1943, this book should be required reading for all accompanists, singers and coaches. Some of the topics covered include partnership, preparation, practicing, rehearsing, performance and bad habits. Other titles by this author include *Am I Too Loud?*, *Farewell Recital (Further Memoirs)*, *Careers in Music*, *Singer and Accompanist: The Performance of Fifty Songs*, and *The Schubert Song Cycles.* As enjoyable to read as they are informative.

4.30   Price, Deon Nielson. *Accompanying Skills for Pianists.* 152 pp. Culver City, CA: Culver Crest Publications, 1991.

The text focuses on these different skills: pianistic, listening, responsive, stylistic, rehearsal and performance. Numerous, useful musical examples.

4.31   Spillman, Robert. *The Art of Accompanying: Master Lessons from the Repertoire.* 368 pp. New York: Schirmer Books, 1985.

A textbook for the student of accompanying. The author spells out the main points covered: development of the ear; concepts of form and direction in the music; how to analyze the music being performed; examples of various kinds of repertoire; rehearsal techniques; cooperation in performance; and a general philosophy of performance. Fourteen units, with accompanying musical examples interspersed among the units. Short bibliography.

5

Discographies and Videographies

Discographies

5.1   Blyth, Alan. *Opera on CD: The Essential Guide to the Best CD Recordings of 100 Operas.* Rev. and updated 3rd. ed. 211 pp. London: Kyle Cathie, Ltd., 1994.

Beginning with Monteverdi and ending with Harrison Birtwistle, lists the author's choices for significant opera recordings. There is also a chapter devoted to collections and recitals. The author, a critic for *Gramophone* magazine, has also compiled the following similar discographies: *Opera on Record* (Hutchinson, 1979); *Opera on Record 2* (Hutchinson, 1983); and the American edition *Opera on Record 3* (Longwood Press, 1984).

5.2   Blyth, Alan. *Song on Record.* 2 vols. Cambridge, England: Cambridge University Press, 1987-88.

A collection of essays written by renowned critics, arranged by composer. Volume 1 is devoted to Lieder while Volume 2 offers information of a more general nature.

5.3   Fellers, Frederick P. *The Metropolitan Opera on Record: A Discography of the Commercial Recordings.* 101 pp. Westport, Conn.: Greenwood Press, 1984. (Discographies, no. 9)

Arranged chronologically by recording session beginning in 1906 and ending in 1972. There are composer and performer indexes.

5.4   Friedwald, Will. *Jazz Singing*. 505 pp. New York: Da Capo, 1996.

A basic history but the key element is a solid discography

5.5   Gänzl, Kurt *The Blackwell Guide to the Musical Theatre on Record.*
         547 pp.   Oxford; Cambridge, Mass.: Blackwell Reference, 1990.
         (Blackwell Reference)

The author selects his personal choices for the top one hundred musicals from
the days of Gilbert & Sullivan and continental operetta to the 1980s. He devotes
ten chapters to his choices of the best recordings of ten shows, along with a list
of "My Ten Essential Records" and "Other Recommended Recordings" at the end
of each. Informative and entertaining reading.

5.6   Gammond, Peter. *Opera on Compact Disc: A Critical Guide to the
         Best Recordings*. 175 pp. New York: Harmony Books, 1987.

Covers more than sixty-eight composers and includes listings of collections on
CD. Also included is Gammond's list of the one hundred best CD recordings.

5.7   Gammond, Peter. *The Illustrated Encyclopedia of Recorded Opera*. 256
         pp. London: Salamander, 1979.

Brief entries on operas by 155 composers, arranged alphabetically. There is also
a biographical guide to 100 opera singers.

5.8   Gruber, Paul. *The Metropolitan Opera Guide to Recorded Opera*. 782
         pp. New York: W. W. Norton & Company, Inc., 1993.

A guide to CD recordings of operas included in the Met's repertoire.

5.9   Hodgins, Gordon W.   *The Broadway Musical: A Complete LP
         Discography*. 183 pp. Metuchen, N. J.: The Scarecrow Press, Inc.,
         1980.

Alphabetical listing by title. Indexed by composer, book and lyrics, performer,
song, composer-lyricist, and major record company sequential index.

5.10   Hummel, David. *The Collector's Guide to the American Musical Theatre*. New revised, enlarged edition. 2 vols. Metuchen, N. J.: The Scarecrow Press, 1984.

First published in 1978 and 1978.   Arranged by title of show, Volume 1 provides extensive information on each and there are essays on British, Australian and Canadian musical theater. Volume 2 is an index.

5.11   Lynch, Richard Chigley. *Broadway on Record: A Directory of New York Cast Recordings of Musical Shows, 1931-1986*. 347 pp. New York: Greenwood Press, 1987. (Discographies, 28)

A listing of commercially-available recordings of both Broadway and Off-Broadway original cast albums.   Includes 459 recordings and approximately 6,000 songs. Entries are arranged alphabetically by show title and include the opening night date and theater. Songs are listed in the order performed in the show and the singers performing each number are listed.   The author also includes a chronological listing of the shows and indexes by performer and a "Technical Index" for composers, lyricists and directors.

5.12   Lynch, Richard Chigley. *Movie Musicals on Record: A Directory of Recordings of Motion Picture Musicals, 1927-1987*. 445 pp. New York: Greenwood, 1989. (Discographies, no. 32)

Similar volumes by Lynch are *Movie Musicals on Record: A Directory of Recordings of Motion Picture Musicals, 1927-1987* (Greenwood Press, 1989); *TV and Studio Cast Musicals on Record: A Discography of Television Musicals and Studio Recordings of Stage and Film Musicals* (Greenwood Press, 1990) and most recently *Broadway, Movie, TV, and Studio Cast Musicals on Record: A Discography of Recordings, 1985-1995* (Greenwood, 1996).

5.13   March, Ivan. *The Penguin Guide to Compact Discs and Cassettes*. New ed., rev. and updated. 1,580 pp. London; New York: Penguin Books, 1996.

This guide is published every two years and lists virtually everything currently in print.

5.14   Miletich, Leo N. *Broadway's Prize-winning Musicals: An Annotated Guide for Libraries and Collectors.* 255 pp. New York: Haworth Press, 1993. (Haworth library and information science)

Intended to present an overall history of the musical through the productions listed. The text is divided into four sections or "acts", three of which cover those musicals that were awarded either Tony, New York Drama Critics Circle Award or the Pulitzer Prize. The fourth section includes musicals that have been selected to due their relevance to the development of the genre, their popularity or their availability. Helpful appendixes are included and there is a song index as well as a general index.

5.15   *OPERA 75: The 75 Greatest Opera Recordings of All Time.* 96 pp. Harrow, Middlesex, Great Britain: Gramophone Publications, 1997.

The seventy-five best opera recordings, according to the reviewers from *Gramophone*.

5.16   Raymond, Jack. *Show Music on Record; the First 100 Years.* 429 pp. Washington, D. C.: Smithsonian Institution Press, 1992.

Chronological listing of all original cast commercial recordings of shows, whether stage, television, or screen. There are also listings of artist and anthology albums.

5.17   Rosenberg, Kenyon C. *A Basic Classical and Operatic Recordings Collection on Compact Disc for Libraries.* 375 pp. Metuchen, N. J.: The Scarecrow Press, 1990.

There is also an earlier edition, published by Scarecrow in 1987, *A Basic Classical and Operatic Recordings Collection for Libraries.*

5.18   Scott, Michael. *The Record of Singing.* Reprint ed. Boston: Northeastern University Press, 1993.

Originally published in two volumes by Duckworth in 1977. Spanning the years from the first recordings made to 1925 and written in conjunction with the recordings issued by EMI under the same title. Entries for hundreds of singers, with photos, introductory essay on singing, glossaries, bibliographies and useful indexes.

5.19   Stahl, Dorothy. *A Selected Discography of Solo Song: Supplement. 1975-1982*. 236 pp. Detroit: Information Coordinators, 1984. (Detroit studies in music bibliography, 52)

A listing of songs in recorded anthologies.   First published in 1968. Supplemented in 1970. Following that, a cumulative volume (through 1971) was published in 1972 and one additional supplement, spanning 1971-1974, was published in 1976.

5.20   Steane, J. B. *The Grand Tradition: Seventy Years of Singing on Record, 1900 to 1970*. 2nd ed. 628 pp. Portland, Ore.: Amadeus, 1993.

The author, a critic for *Gramophone*, traces the history of vocal music on record from Patti to Domingo, with discussion on one hundred singers in total.   There is also a chapter on choral music. Many photographs. The first edition was published in 1974. In the preface to this edition, the author promises a second volume.

5.21   Turner, Patricia. *Dictionary of Afro-American Performers: 78 rpm and Cylinder Recordings of Opera, Choral Music and Song, c. 1900-1949*. 433 pp. New York: Garland, 1990. (Garland reference library of the humanities, 590)

Includes biographical information on the performers, along some bibliographical entries.   Provides some information about collections around the country, spirituals, compositions by African Americans, and other useful facts. Readers may also consult the author's *Afro-American Singers: An Index and Preliminary Discography of Long-Playing Recordings of Opera, Choral Music and Song*, published in 1977 by Challenge Productions.

Videographies

5.22   Almquist, Sharon G.   *Opera Mediagraphy: Video Recordings and Motion Pictures*. 269 pp. Westport, Conn.: Greenwood Press, 1994. (Music reference collection, 40)

Provides a listing of performances of over 150 operas. Indexes for singers, composers, conductors, and locations of productions.

5.23   Blyth, Alan. *Opera on Video: The Essential Guide.* 246 pp. London Kyle Cathie, 1995.

Lists 100 operas by forty composers. Theatrical releases not included (e.g. Zeffirelli's *Otello*).

5.24   Croissant, Charles. *Opera Performances in Video Format: A Checklist of Commercially Released Recordings.* 121 pp. Canton, Mass.: Music Library Association, 1991. (MLA Index and Bibliography Series Number 26)

Arranged alphabetically by composer.

5.25   Gruber, Paul. *The Metropolitan Opera Guide to Opera on Video.* 483 pp. New York: Norton, 1997.

Videography of over 150 operas, indexes to performers and directors.

5.26   Levine, Robert and the editors of Consumer Reports Books. *Guide to Opera and Dance on Videocassette.* 224 pp. Mt. Vernon, N. Y.: Consumers Union,1900.

The author's intent is to provide the reader with the background necessary to make intelligent selections when purchasing or renting videos. 175 videos included, with 115 of them being opera productions.

5.27   Wlaschin, Ken. *Opera on Screen: A Guide to 100 Years of Films and Videos Featuring Operas, Opera Singers, and Operettas.* 628 pp. + computer optical laser disc. Los Angeles, Calif.: Beachwood Press, 1997.

A dictionary guide to film and video versions of operas and operettas.

6

Pedagogical Resources

6.1   Alderson, Richard. *Complete Book of Voice Training.* 255 pp. Englewood Cliffs, N. J.: Parker Publishing Company Inc., 1979.

Written by a voice teacher who is also a choral director, the main focus of this book is on the young singer. In addition to the usual chapters on breathing, resonance, vowels, diction, and interpretation, the author includes chapters on choral singing, voice classes, and the changing voice.

6.2   Appelman, Dudley Ralph. *The Science of Vocal Pedagogy: Theory and Application.* 1st Midland ed. 434 pp. Bloomington: Indiana University Press, 1986.

First published in 1967. There are accompanying sound recordings (three cassettes or five lps) for this first edition. Appelman states in his preface that there are four objectives for this book: "to intentionally and directly train the singer's aural awareness of his vocal utterance of the word," "the description of the scientific theories of vocal pedagogy," "to suggest a system of vocal pedagoy based upon the International Phonetic Alphabet," and the "establishement of an acoustical model of phonemic utterance that may be accepted as a standard for imitation." Designed to be used as a textbook, it is an absolute basic to the study of vocal pedagogy.

6.3   Ardoin, John. *Callas at Juilliard: The Master Classes.* 300 pp. New York: Alfred A. Knopf, 1987.

Mr. Ardoin, music critic and columnist, is primarily responsible for the many books written about Maria Callas. In this text, he has organized the transcripts from the diva's master classes at Juilliard into a very helpful resource for operatic singers. Repertoire from forty-four operas is treated within these pages. There is a prologue built from her comments throughout the classes and from interviews granted by Callas. Included also is a glossary. Many musical examples.

6.4   Brown, Oren L. *Discover Your Voice: How to Develop Healthy Voice Habits.* 286 pp. + CD. San Diego, Calif.: Singular Publishing Group Inc., 1996.

Noted voice teacher and voice therapist begins his treatise with the primal voice and goes from there in this detailed study of singing and vocal health.

6.5   Butenschon, Sine, and Hans M. Borchgrevink. *Voice and Song.* 62 pp. Cambridge: Cambridge University Press, 1982.

First published in Norway as *Stemme og sang* (Dreyer) in 1978. Explains the *dorsal method* of singing, which according to the authors, produces sensations in the back of the singer's body, when properly executed.

6.6   Caldwell, J. Timothy. *Expressive Singing: Dalcroze Eurhythmics for Voice.* 177 pp. Englewood Cliffs, N. J.: Prentice-Hall, 1995.

Based on the premise that incorporating the use of vocal expression into the teaching of technique will enhance the learning experience, Caldwell examines Dalcroze's philosophy and methodology and applies them to vocal study. He asserts that the whole body is involved in the learning process. The book is divided into three parts. The first, 'Background,' discusses why the author turned to Dalcroze in the study of performance and also provides information on Dalcroze and his philosophy on teaching. The second offers Dalcroze's methods. The third shows the reader how to put the methodologies to work. Appendixes include exercises for learning music and a voice registration chart.

6.7   Coffin, Berton. *Sounds of Singing: Vocal Techniques with Vowel-pitch Charts.* 2nd ed. 308 pp. Metuchen, N. J.: The Scarecrow Press, 1987.

Emphasizes the use of vowel resonance in singing.

6.8   Coffin, Berton. *Overtones of Bel Canto: Phonetic Basis of Artistic Singing with 100 Chromatic Vowel Chart Exercises.*   236 pp. Metuchen, N. J.: The Scarecrow Press, 1980.

In the Foreword, the author states the purpose of this book: "...to set forth in acoustic phonetics, register and musical notation, many exercises which will collect and make the voice strong and more musical according to the precepts of Bel Canto." (p. ix)

6.9   Cummings, Henry. *Take a Deep Breath: A Comprehensive Guide to the Working of the Singer's Voice.* 112 pp. London: Thames Pub., 1993.

6.10   David, Marilee. *The New Voice Pedagogy.* 217 pp. Lanham, Md.: Scarecrow Press, 1995.

Seven chapters that cover the larynx, posture and relaxation, sound and tone quality, registration and placement, ethics, etc. There is a glossary of terms.

6.11   Fields, Victor A. *Foundations of the Singer's Art.* 118 pp. New York: The National Association of Teachers of Singing, Inc., 1984.

First published in 1977 by Vantage (New York). The first volume of NATS' *Heritage Series of Pedagogical Classics.* Prof. Fields taught diction and voice at the City College of New York for over forty years and was a charter member of NATS. Readers should also consult his other books *The Singers' Glossary* and *Training the Singing Voice.* This particular book presents his philosophies and techniques for vocal study.

6.12   Foote, Jeffrey. *The Vocal Performer: Development Through Science and Imagery.* 166 pp. Weidman, Mich.: Wildwood Music, 1992.

A good place to locate vocal exercises.

6.13   Gardiner, Julian. *A Guide to Good Singing and Speech.* 300 pp. Boston: Crescendo Publishing Company, 1972.

Previously published by Cassell & Company, Ltd. (London) in 1968. This English proponent of *bel canto* offers his approach to singing. There are many photographs showing various examples of vowel shapes, tongue placement, and so forth. The author's friendly approach includes suggestions to remove flowers from rooms where singing is to occur and to fight laryngitis with "philosophic fortitude" or with "a new hat, good food, and an afternoon cinema."

6.14   Giles, Peter. *The History and Technique of the Counter-Tenor.* 459 pp. Aldershot, England: Scolar Press, 1994.

Divided into two large sections, those being "The History of the Counter-Tenor" and "The Technique of the Counter-Tenor." Numerous appendixes, a general index and a glossary of vocal terms compiled by Charels Cleall. Interested readers should also consult the author's previous studies *The Counter-Tenor* (1982) and *A Basic Counter-Tenor Method* (1988).

6.15   Halbert, Marjorie. *Releasing the Inner Voice: A Guide for Singers.* 127 pp. + cassette. Brentwood, Tenn.: ISI Publishing, 1996.

A combination workbook, "how-to," and singer's diary. Covers posture, breathing, vocal health, practice methods, and includes some vocalises and a cassette tape of accompaniments for them.

6.16   Hammar, Russell A. *Singing: An Extension of Speech.* 208 pp. Metuchen, N. J.: The Scarecrow Press, 1978.

In his introduction, the author states that the main point of this book is "to emphasize that good tone in speech or in singing is made through pure vowel production" (p. 6). Chapter topics include the importantance of the vowel in vocal production, the anatomy of the vocal mechanism, the passaggio and the falsetto, consonants, breathing and posture, teaching aids and interpretation.

6.17   Herbert-Caesari, Edgar F. *The Voice of the Mind.* 366 pp. Boston, Mass.: Crescendo Publishing Company, 1971.

First published in 1951 by Robert Hale & Company, London. Herbert-Caesari was a strong advocate for the study of *bel canto*. This study is a partner to his *The Science and Sensations of Vocal Tone* (Dent, 1936).

6.18   Herbert-Caesari, Edgar F. *Vocal Truth: Some of the Things I Teach.* 110 pp. Boston: Crescendo Publishing Company; London: Robert Hale & Company, 1970.

The subtitle explains the context of this small volume.

6.19   Hewitt, Graham. *How to Sing.* 94 pp. London: Elm Tree Books, 1978.

Most helpful for the beginning student of voice, especially in regards to diction and how to practice.

6.20   Hewlett, Arthur D. *Think Afresh about the Voice.* 60 pp. London: The Ernest George White Society, 1970.

Hewlett, a student of E.G. White's, offers a reassessment of White's theories and teachings about sinus tone production.

6.21   Jones, Earl William. *Sound, Self, and Song: Essays on the Teaching of Singing.* 231 pp. Metuchen, N. J.: Scarecrow Press, 1989.

A collection of eleven essays by the author on pedagogy and voice.

6.22   Leyerle, William D. *Vocal Development Through Organic Imagery.* 2nd ed., revised and enlarged. 177 pp. Geneseo, New York: Leyerle Publications, 1986.

The author's method of singing is outlined in twelve chapters. Includes nine appendixes and many illustrations.

6.23   McKinney, James C. *The Diagnosis and Correction of Vocal Faults.*
        Rev. and expanded ed.   212 pp. and cassette tape. Nashville, Tenn.:
        Genevox Music Group, 1994.

The subtitle of this book is "a manual for teachers of singing and choir
directors." It is designed to aid in the analysis of vocal problems that can be
resolved in the studio or rehearsal hall. Its size and organization make it an easy-
to-use resource.

6.24   Manén, Lucien.   *Bel Canto: The Teaching of the Classical Italian
        Song-schools; Its Decline and Restoration.*   76 pp. Oxford: Oxford
        University Press, 1987.

One of the newest examinations of the bel canto style, written by a singer and
voice teacher, who was the first "Cherubino" at Glyndebourne.   There is a
bibliography.   Also published in German as *Bel Canto: die Lehre der
Klassischen Italienischen Gesangschulen,*   Heinrichschofen (Wilhelmshaven,
1986).

6.25   Miller, Richard.   *National Schools of Singing: English, French,
        German and Italian Techniques of Singing revisited.*   Revised edition.
        237 pp. Metuchen, N. J.: Scarecrow, 1997.

Examines all aspects of singing and of the vocal apparatus in light of national
schools of singing. Extensive bibliography and index.

6.26   Miller, Richard. *On the Art of Singing.* 318 pp. New York: Oxford
        University Press, 1996.

Previously published essays, some revised.   Of the ninety-five essays, the
majority were originally published in *The NATS Journal.*   The essays are
separated into these categories: "On training the singing voice," "On musical
style and interpretation," "On preparation for the professional life," and "On the
singing voice and vocal function."

6.27   Miller, Richard. *The Structure of Singing: System and Art in Vocal
        Technique.* 372 pp. New York: Schirmer Books, 1986.

Prof. Miller's treatise on singing. Includes many musical examples and plenty of illustrations of various components of the singing mechanism. Useful glossaries and bibliographies. Yet another important text by Prof. Miller is *Training Tenor Voices* (Schrimer Books, 1993).

6.28   Newsom, Brad. *The Athletics of Voice.* 107 pp. Hawthorne, Calif: New Wind Press, 1994.

This is a basic pedagogy of singing, based on the teachings of Erwin Windward, who sudied medicine and team sports before he became a voice teacher. His method employs the philosophy that singing is an athletic activity and should be pursued as such.

6.29   Phillips, Kenneth H. *Teaching Kids to Sing.* 392 pp. New York; London: Schirmer Books; Prentice Hall Iinternational, 1996.

Chapter titles include "Vocal Pedagogy for Young Singers," "The Psychomotor Process," "Vocal Parameters," "The Child and Adolscent Singer," "The Healthy Voice," and chapters on technique and curriculum, respiration, phonation, tone, diction and expression.

6.30   Reid, Cornelius L. *The Free Voice.* 225 pp. New York: Joseph Patelson Music House, 1971.

Previously published in 1965 by Coleman-Ross Company, Inc. Reid discusses his own particular teaching style and philosophy. Other books by him include *Bel Canto: Principles and Practice* (Patelson, 1972 reprint); *Voice: Psyche and Soma* (Patelson, 1975) and *Essays on the Nature of Singing* (Recital Publications, 1993). See also 1.43: *A Dictionary of Vocal Terminology: An Analysis.*

6.31   Salaman, Esther. *Unlocking Your Voice: Freedom to Sing.* 133 pp. London: Gollancz, 1989.

A student of Lucien Manén who is now a professor emeritus of the Guildhall School of Music, Salaman discusses her own teaching method, performance tension, vocal strain, choral singing, and the teacher/sudent relationship, among other topics.

6.32   Tibbetts, George Richard. *The Vocal Pedagogy Index 1996.* 2 vols.
        Philadelphia, Penn.: The Institute for the Psychological & Pedagogical
        Study of Voice Performance, 1996.

Lists books, scores, media and periodical articles for vocal pedagogy and related
areas. Also includes reviews from the *Journal of Singing* in the last five years
and in the *Journal of Voice.*

6.33   Vennard, William. *Developing Voices.* 60 pp. New York: Carl
        Fischer, 1973.

This small booklet accompanies a set of sound recordings which illustrate
specific vocal problems. The booklet is divided into three sections: "An Outline
of Comparative Pedagogy," "The Psychology of the Pupil-Teacher
Relationship," and "Notes from the Accompanying Recordings." Another very
important text that must be included, regardless of copyright date is this author's
Singing: The Mechanism and Technic. (Fifth edition. Carl Fischer, 1967).
Vennard was a voice teacher, whose first edition of this study appeared in 1949.
He was the chair of the voice department at the University of Southern
California and Past President of NATS at the time of publication of the revised
edition. A very straight-forward study of the vocal mechanism and the related
principles that create a sound technique. Includes an extensive bibliography, a
thesaurus and an index that uses paragraph numbers, rather than page numbers.

6.34   Wormhoudt, Pearl Shinn. *Building the Voice as an Instrument.*
        193 pp. Oskaloosa, IA: William Penn College, 1981.

Covers all aspects of vocal pedagogy, along with chapters on learning new
repertoire, singing in large ensembles, programming and care of the voice. Also
includes a "Singer's Reference Handbook" that includes a summary of vocal
exercises recommended and used by the author, a sample student record sheet, the
IPA, guides for foreign language diction, a listing of song anthologies arranged
by publisher, names and addresses of publishers, professional organizations, a
glossary and a bibliography organized to correspond to certain chapters. In its
sixth printing, with additions on tension release, body management, vowel
resonance and stage fright.

6.35   Young, Arabella Hong. *Singing Professionally: Studying Singing for
        Actors and Singers.* 129 pp. Portsmouth, N. H.: Heinemann, 1995.

Ms. Hong Young was the first Helen Chiao in *The Flower Drum Sung* on Broadway and has been a voice teacher and performer for over 30 years. Her book defines a pedagogy for singing musical theater using the more traditional classical approach to technique. Along with chapters on the mechanics of singing and auditioning, she includes chapters on adapting the operatic voice into the musical theater styles and on the Zen of singing. Readers interested in learning more about alternative philosophies of pedagogy might want to read *The Tao of Voice: A New East-West Approach to Transforming the Singing and Speaking Voice* by Stephen Chun-Tao Cheng (Destiny Books, 1991).

Class Voice

6.36   Christy, Van Ambrose, and John Glenn Paton.   *Foundations in Singing: A Basic Text in Vocal Technique and Song Interpretation.* 6th edition. 292 pp. Madison, Wis.: Brown & Benchmark, 1997.

A long-standing text for both class voice and private study. Combines both a text on the study of singing and an anthology of songs. Several helpful appendixes.

6.37   Harpster, Richard W. *Technique in Singing: A Program for Singers and Teachers.* 136 pp. New York: Schirmer Books, 1984.

Conveniently designed for a fifteen-week course of vocal study, complete with study questions and exercises.

6.38   Kenney, James. *Becoming a Singing Performer: A Text for Voice Classes.* 249 pp. Dubuque, Iowa: Wm. C. Brown Publishers, 1987.

Text for class study, an anthology, reading and listening lists, and a glossary all geared towards the beginning student.

6.39   Lightner, Helen. *Class Voice and the American Art Song: A Source Book and Anthology.* 181 pp. Metuchen, N. J.: The Scarecrow Press, 1991.

Divided into three parts, this text provides a unit of procedures for devising and conducting a voice class, a unit of vocal training, and an anthology of thirty-two songs.   The author, a voice teacher, includes biographical essays on each composer represented as well as comments regarding stylistic features of the music.   There is a brief bibliography and an index.

6.40   Lindsley, Charles Edward.   *Fundamentals for Singing.*   264 pp. Belmont, Calif.: Wadsworth Publishing Company, 1985.

Both textbook and song anthology for beginning class voice.   Provides basic information about the physiology of the voice, vocal exercises and an anthology of nearly forty selections, many of them in both high and low keys.   Many illustrations of the vocal apparatus. There is a bibliography but no index.

6.41   Miller, Kenneth E.   *Principles of Singing: A Textbook for First-Year Singers.*   196 pp.   Englewood Cliffs, N. J.: Prentice-Hall, Inc., 1983.

Discussion of the various aspects of beginning vocal study spread over seventeen chapters along with thirty-seven songs for study.   Chapter topics include, to name a few, "Self-Consciousness," "Posture and Singing," "Singing with a Free Tone," and "Registers."

6.42   Sable, Barbara Kinsey. *The Vocal Sound.* 149 pp. Englewood Cliffs, N. J.: Prentice-Hall, Inc., 1982.

Written to support vocal study, either in the studio or the classroom, and with the intent to provide sufficient information on a variety of related topics so that the teacher is free to concentrate on singing.   Some of the chapter headings include "The Practice Routine," "Songs and How to Sing Them," "Theory and the Voice Student," and "Listening for the Vocal Sound."

6.43   Schmidt, Jan.   *Basics of Singing.*   Second edition.   286 pp. New York: Schirmer Books, 1989.

Covers basic singing technique, musicianship and interpretation.   Geared primarily towards beginning students. Includes an anthology of fifty-six songs, including several from more recent musical theater productions. The anthology also includes eleven rounds to be used to in the classroom to promote ease and confidence in singing in harmony.   Available separately are tapes of accompaniments, in both high and low keys, for the songs in the anthology.

6.44   Ware, Clifton. *Adventures in Singing: A Process for Exploring, Discovering, and Developing Vocal Potential.* 303 pp. New York: McGraw-Hill, 1995.

Intended for the beginning student in a class setting. Includes more than sixty songs in an anthology. Also includes a large bibliography and two glossaries (musical terms and vocal terms). Cassettes or compact disc recordings of the accompaniments for the included songs are available. The author's *Basics of Vocal Pedagogy: the Foundations and Process of Singing* is expected to be published by McGraw-Hill in 1998.

Historical Resources

6.45   Celletti, Rodolfo. *A History of Bel Canto.* Translated by Frederick Fuller. 218 pp. Oxford: Clarendon Press, 1991.

Chapter headings include "The Cult of Bel Canto, Virtuosity, and Hedonism," "The Vocal Art in Baroque Opera," "Particular Aspects of Baroque Opera," "Rossini," and "Death and Resurrection of Bel Canto." Indexes for names and opera titles.

6.46   Coffin, Berton. *Historical Vocal Pedagogy Classics.* 303 pp. Metuchen, N. J. and London: The Scarecrow Press, 1989.

Professor Coffin's reviews of many of the monuments of vocal pedagogy, including the writings of Tosi, Mancini, García, Marchesi, Lamperti, and Lehmann.

6.47   García, Manuel. *A Complete Treatise on the Art of Singing, Parts One and Two.* 2 vols. Collated, edited and translated by Donald V. Paschke. New York: Da Capo Press, 1984.

García, the inventor of the laryngoscope, combined his knowledge and artistry of *bel canto* singing with a much more scientific approach. This treatise is his testament on the singing art. The original edition first appeared in 1840 as *Traité complet de l'art du chant en deux parties.* He was born into a family of singers; his father was a fine tenor, his sisters, Maria Malibran and Pauline Viardot had distinguished careers and were some of his earliest students. Other famous students include Jenny Lind and Mathilde Marchesi, another famous teacher.

6.48   García, Manuel. *Hints on Singing*. 75 pp. Canoga Park, Calif: Summit Publishing Company, 1970.

Full of musical examples, exercises, and illustrations, this guide for singing is arranged in a question-and-answer format. It covers all aspects of the voice and singing, as well as performance practice. Originally written in French, this particular version was translated by García's grandaughter.

6.49   Hahn, Reynaldo. *On Singers and Singing: Lectures and Essays*. 244 pp. Translated by Léo Simoneau. Portland, Ore.: Amadeus Press, 1990.

A collection of nine lectures given by this French composer between 1912 and 1914. Topics include "Why Do We Sing?," "How Do We Sing?," "How to Enunciate in Singing," and "How to Move an Audience" among others. Interesting reading, not only in regard to singing, but also for gaining a sense of the musical world at that time.

6.50   Marafioti, P. Mario. *Caruso's Method of Voice Production*. 308 pp. New York: Dover, 1981.

Originally published in 1922, in a limited edition of 100 copies by D. Appleton & Co., New York. Marafioti, a laryngologist who worked closely with Caruso and other notable singers of the day, explains to the reader, in scientific terms, what made the tenor's voice what it was. He proposes that what Caruso did instinctively can be learned by other singers. There are many illustrations, as well as x-ray photographs, of vowel formation, a number of vocalises, and most interestingly, photographs of Caruso himself singing the vowels. This important pedagogical monograph was dedicated to Caruso only days before his death.

6.51   Monahan, Brent Jeffrey. *The Art of Singing: A Compendium of Thoughts on Singing Published Between 1777 and 1927*. 342 pp. Metuchen, N. J.: The Scarecrow Press, 1978.

Quotations from vocal pedagogues spanning 150 years, divided among eleven chapters. Features both an annotated and a separate chronological bibliography, along with a bibliography of secondary sources, works that were not included in the study and periodical literature.

6.52   Newton, George. *Sonority in Singing: A Historical Essay.* 146 pp. New York: Vantage Press, Inc., 1984.

Traces the development of singing technique from the Middle Ages forward.

6.53   Tosi, Pier Francisco, ca. 1653-1732. *Opinioni de' Antichi e Moderni (Introduction to the Art of Singing).* By Johann Friedrich Agricola; translated and edited by Julianne C. Baird. 298 pp. Cambridge; New York: Cambridge University Press, 1995. (Cambridge musical texts and monographs)

A translation into English of an early treatise on singing, written by voice teacher and castrato, too. Originally published in 1723, it would later published in German by Agricola in 1757. Agricola's commentary on Tosi's work is historically significant in the study of performance practice. An English translation of Tosi's treatise appeared earlier in 1742 and was the work of J.E. Galliard. Modern-day editions can be found under the title *Observations on the Florid Song.* This English version is edited by Julianne Baird, a highly-respected interpreter of early music. Includes extensive bibliography and index.

Vocal Science

6.54   Brodnitz, Friedrich S. *Keep Your Voice Healthy.* 2nd ed. 158 pp. San Diego, Calif.: College-Hill/Little, Brown and Company, 1988.

The author, a physician, offers a useful handbook on the care of the voice. The first edition was published in 1953.

6.55   Bunch, Meribeth A. *Dynamics of the Singing Voice.* 156 pp. Secaucus, N. J.: Springer-Verlag New York Inc., 1982.

The primary aim of the book is to provide a "meeting ground" for vocal artists and voice scientists and therapists. It is divided into four areas that cover terminology, the process of singing, the function of the voice and how to teach it, and relating function to the art of singing.

6.56   Colton, Raymond H., and Janina K. Caspar. *Understanding Voice Problems: A Physiological Perspective for Diagnosis and Treatment.* 355 pp. Baltimore: Williams and Wilkins, 1990.

Written by otolaryngologists, the text explains that in order to understand vocal problems, one must first understand the proper functions of the mechanism. Chapters cover the study of the larynx, the eight primary symptoms of vocal disorders, vocal abuse due to both neurological and physical causes, voice history, surgery, and rehabilitation.

6.57   Dejonekere, P. H., Minoru Hirano, and John Sundberg. *Vibrato.* 152 pp. San Diego, Calif.: Singular Publishing Group, 1996.

A collection of papers presented at the Congress of the Collegium Medicorum Theatri in Utrecht in August, 1993.

6.58   Fujimura, Osamu and Minoru Hirano. *Vocal Fold Physiology: Voice Quality Control.* 357 pp. San Diego, Calif.: Singular Publishing Group, 1995.

The ninth monograph in the *Vocal Fold Physiology* series produced by The Voice Foundation. Five sections cover phonetics and speech, acoustics and physics, expression and singing, physiology and pathology, and finally an overall discussion that includes a chapter entitled "Definitions and Nomenclature Related to Voice Quality" written by Ingo Titze. Highly clinical.

6.59   Hirano, Minoru. *Clinical Examination of Voice.* 100 pp. Secaucus, N. J.: Springer-Verlag New York, Inc., 1981.

Presents standardized techniques for the examination of the voice.

6.60   Large, John. *Contributions of Voice Research to Singing.* 426 pp. Houston, Tx: College-Hill, 1980.

A collection of articles relating to vocal science in these areas: aerodynamics, vocal registers, vibrato, singers' formants, and intelligibility. Many of the articles were chosen to show the "historical development of original ideas" while others were chosen due to the difficulty of finding to them in most music libraries.

6.61   Morrison, Murray, Linda Rummage, and others. *The Management of Voice Disorders.* 266 pp. San Diego, Calif.: Singular Publishing Group, Inc., 1994.

A systematic approach to the care of the singing voice, written by specialists from one particular vocal clinic.

6.62   Proctor, Donald F. *Breathing, Speech and Song.* 176 pp. Secaucus, N. J.: Springer-Verlag New York Inc., 1980.

A discussion of the physiology of singing and speaking and the effect of proper breathing on both.

6.63   Sataloff, Robert T. *Professional Voice: The Science and Art of Clinical Care.* 527 pp. New York: Raven Press, 1991.

Along with fourteen contributors, the author has assembled an overview of the study of voice. There are thirty-three chapters that cover an obviously wide range of topics.

6.64   Sataloff, Robert T., and Ingo R. Titze. *Vocal Health and Science.* 289 pp. Jacksonville, Fla.: NATS, 1991.

A collection of eighty-nine articles from *The NATS Bulletin* and *The NATS Journal.*

6.65   Sundberg, Johan. *The Science of the Singing Voice.* 216 pp. De Kalb, IL: Northern Illinois University Press, 1987.

The author's own translation of his original monograph, *Röstlära.* An examination of the singing voice versus the speaking voice and a look at the research associated with it. As the title implies, this is a much more scientifically-based study, using the terminology of medicine and acoustics, rather than that of the voice studio. Extensive bibliography and index.

6.66 Titze, Ingo R. *Principles of Voice Production.* 354 pp. Englewood Cliffs, N. J.: Prentice-Hall, Inc., 1994.

Comprehensive and highly clinical examination of vocal production.

Jazz and Pop

6.67 Allen, Jeffrey Lee. *Jeffrey Allen's Secrets of Singing.* Female edition (Low and High Voice). 377 pp. + 2 compact discs. Miami, Fla. CPP/Belwin, Inc., 1996. Male edition (Low and High Voice). 376 pp. + 2 compact discs.

Basic pedagogical information with a pop-style slant to it. The text is comprised of thirty-two chapters within five major sections. The accompanying CDs contain a selection of vocal exercises. No clear pedagogical distinction is discernable between the two editions regarding male voices versus female voices, or low versus high.

6.68 Coker, Patty, and David N. Baker. *Vocal Improvisation: An Instrumental Approach.* 148 pp + cassette. Lebanon, Ind.: Studio P/R, 1981.

By utilizing many of the proven instrumental improvisational techniques, the authors have assembled a logical course of training for the vocalist, beginning with intervals and proceeding to scales, chord-scale relationships, etc. Sample chapter headings include "Psychology of the Singer," "Vocalise - Vocal-Ease," and "Learning and Internalizing a Tune."

6.69 Fredrickson, Scott. *Scat Singing Method.* 88 pp. + 2 cassettes. Hollywood, Calif.; Sherman Oaks, Calif.: Scott Music Publications; sole selling agent, Alfred Pub. Co., 1982.

Step-by-step instructions for the beginning jazz vocalist.

6.70   Lyons, Jodie and Lanelle Stevenson. *P. O. P. S.: Principles of Pop Singing*. 301 pp. New York: Schirmer Books, 1990.

The purpose of this book is to provide a sound pedagogical approach to all styles of pop singing: rock, country, jazz and swing. Along with vocal techniques, the book includes discussion of basic harmony. Appendixes cover IPA, listening lists for all four styles, chord symbols, a glossary and a bibliography. Full of musical examples, both within the text and on an accompanying cassette.

6.71   Tormé, Mel. *My Singing Teachers*. 228 pp. New York; Oxford: Oxford University Press, 1994.

The "Velvet Fog" pays homage to those artists who served as his models and mentors throughout his career, including Bessie Smith, Billie Holiday, Tony Bennett, Bing Crosby, Louis Armstong, Ella Fitzgerald and many more. Chatty, very entertaining reading.

7

Stage Resources

7.1   Alper, Steven M. *Next! : Auditioning for the Musical Theater.* 105 pp. Portsmouth, N.H.: Heinemann, 1995.

A useful "how-to" for anyone preparing for auditions. Full of humor and sometimes painfully vivid anecdotes, the book takes the reader through every aspect of the audition, provides definitions of terms throughout the text, and includes an appendix that offers suggestions for repertoire building. The author's e-mail address is also listed.

7.2   Balk, H. Wesley. *The Complete Singer-actor: Training for Music Theater.* Second edition. 251 pp. Minneapolis, Minn: University of Minnesota Press, 1985.

First published in 1977. Presents a synergistic approach to performance for the singer-actor. Another book by the same author is *Performing Power: a New Approach for the Singer-actor* (University of Minnesota Press, 1985).

7.3   *Career Guide for Singers 1996-97.* 202 pp. Washington, D. C.: Opera America, 1996.

Published every two years, this guide provides a wealth of information on everything from places to receive advanced training, either in workshops or institutes, major opera workshops, places that offers degrees in opera or performance, competitions and grants. There is an alphabetical index as well as a geographical one. *A Singer's Guide to the Professional Opera Companies*, also published by Opera America, 1989, is equally helpful.

7.4   Craig, David. *A Performer Prepares: A Guide to Song Preparation for Actors, Singers, and Dancers.* 311 pp. New York: Applause Books, 1993. (The Applause acting series)

The third book written by Craig for performers (see *On Singing Onstage* and *On Performing*). In this volume, the author offers the reader "coachings" on thirteen categories of musical theater repertoire. Each category includes an explanation of that particular category (show ballad, patter song, showstopper, etc.), brief list of titles of songs, a particular song in lead sheet form to be used in the "coaching," and a fictional dialogue between the author and student that leads to a final finished product for that session.

7.5   Craig, David. *On Performing; A Handbook for Actors, Dancers, Singers on the Musical Stage.* 298 pp. New York: McGraw - Hill Book Company, 1987

The author, a long-time coach and teacher of singing, looks at the business of getting into "the business" by examining the concept of style, the audition process, and the "twenty most often asked questions" and his answers. These questions address problems such as "How do I get past technique and begin to surrender to the music?" and "How can I get an Equity card if I haven't worked and the only way I can work is if I have an Equity card?" Perhaps the most informative and interesting portion of the book is the chapter containing transcriptions of interviews with some leading stars of the stage and film, including Bernadette Peters, Robert Preston, Lena Horne, Richard Kiley, Tony Roberts, Gene Kelly, Nancy Walker, George Hearn, and Lee Remick.

7.6   Craig, David. *On Singing Onstage.* 209 pp. New and completely revised edition. New York: Applause Theatre Book Publishers, 1989.

The book is geared mostly towards the actor and the dancer, although anyone preparing to embark on a career in musical theater will find it helpful.

7.7   *Directory of Sets, Costumes, and Title Projections.* 140 pp. Washington, D. C.: Opera America, 1994.

Lists availability of sets, props, costumes, title projections, and related music materials for opera productions. Detailed information down to height of tallest set piece and number of crew members needed for load-in and production. It is noted in the introduction that since the data is maintained by Opera America in computerized format, it can be printed and sorted in a made-to-order fashion and that inquiries are encouraged. Also includes the 1994 set and costume registry from the National Alliance for Musical Theatre. Opera America provides other helpful directories including *Directory of American and Foreign Contemporary Opera and Music Theatre Works, 1980-1989* and *Directory of Opera Education Programs*. To learn about more of Opera America's many publication, readers should visit the website at [http://www.operaam.org/].

7.8   Dornemann, Joan, and Maria Ciaccia. *Complete Preparation: A Guide to Auditioning for Opera*. 149 pp. New York: Excalibur, 1992.

Dornemann, whose home base of operation is the Met, is one of the world's leading opera coaches. Ciaccia is a former student of hers. The book offers valuable insights in what it takes to be a professional singer. It is straightforward in its style and discusses everything involved in the preparation for a professional career from picking the appropriate repertoire and appropriate appearance to appropriate professional behavior.

7.9   Dunsby, Jonathan. *Performing Music: Shared Concerns*. 112 pp. Oxford: Clarendon Press, 1995.

The author, himself a pianist and professor of music, explores the various aspects of musical performance. Written from the pianist's standpoint, there is still considerable information for the singing performer -- or any performer, for that matter. Bibliography included.

7.10   Edwards, Geoffrey and Ryan Edwards. *The Verdi Baritone: Studies in the Development of Dramatic Character*. 193 pp. Bloomington: Indiana University Press, 1994.

The former Edwards, a stage director, along with the latter, a Verdi baritone, examine the significance of this particular role in *Nabucco, Ernani, Macbeth, Rigoletto, La Traviata, Simon Boccanegra*, and *Otello*. Appendixes provide synopses for all seven operas.

7.11   Green, Ruth M. *The Wearing of Costume.* 171 pp. New York: Drama Publishers, 1995.

Originally published by Pitman in 1966. Discusses costume from Roman Britain through World War II as well as how to wear the costumes and how to move in them. Includes many illustrations.

7.12   Helfgot, Daniel, with William O. Beeman. *The Third Line: The Opera Performer as Interpreter.* 242 pp. New York: Schirmer Books; Toronto: Maxwell Macmillan Canada, 1993.

The authors' purpose is to point out the many things singers must know to establish themselves in the operatic world. At the core of this guide is the "third line," the interpretive line the performer adds to both the lines of text and of music. Chapters focus on a variety of topics to be considered by operatic singers: strong minds and bodies, acting ability, movement and expression, interpretive problems, polished performances, the roles of both the voice teacher and the vocal coach, auditions, competitions and recitals. There is also a bibliography of resources for opera in an appendix that includes useful annotations.

7.13   Kislan, Richard. *The Musical: A Look at the American Musical Theater.* 310 pp. New York: Applause, 1995.

An introductory survey that covers four areas: history via the musical form; the contributions of Kern, Rogers and Hammerstein and Sondheim; and the major elements that comprise the musical (book, lyrics, score, dance, design) and recent trends in the business. Originally published in 1980 by Prentice-Hall.

7.14   Kornick, Rebecca Hodell. *Recent American Opera: A Production Guide.* 352 pp. New York: Columbia University Press, 1991.

Provides access to over 200 American operas and musical theater productions. Most of the works were premiered after 1972 although some were included in Eaton's *Opera Production I* and *II*. Listings of musical theater productions are included to correspond to the inclusion of them in opera companies' seasons. Individual entries include a descriptive paragraph of the opera, first performances, recordings, and the like. An overview of the plot is included along with production requirements and reviews. There is a listing of publishers, a title index and an index for productions running less than ninety minutes in length.

7.15   Kosarin, Oscar. *The Singing Actor: How to be a Success in Musical Theater and Nightclubs.* 190 pp. Englewood Cliffs, N.J.: Prentice-Hall, Inc., 1983.

The author states in the preface that there are certain universal qualities that all singing performers share that mark a successful performance: a high energy level; personal involvement in the song; a strong sense of reality; communication with the audience; and the unique personal qualities of the performer. This book offers suggestions to the performer to enhance these qualities through a variety of exercises and ideas. Divided into four parts, the book covers such areas as "The Song as Drama," "Voice and Diction," "The Body and Movement," and "Nightclubs." Appendixes include discussions of relaxation, anxiety, breathing exercises, and posture. There is a bibiliography.

7.16   Laughlin, Haller and Randy Wheeler. *Producing the Musical: A Guide for School, College, and Community Theatres.* 151 pp. Westport, Conn.: Greenwood Press, 1984.

Written for those involved with amateur theater groups. Divided into three large chapters, the first of which covers the business aspects of producing a musical, the second being an annotated listing of some 300 musicals, the basic requirements and the companies that control production rights, and the third being a directory of sources needed for productions. Short glossary of theater terminology, a short bibliography and an index.

7.17   Legge, Anthony. *The Art of Auditioning: A Handbook for Singers, Accompanists and Coaches.* Revised edition. 194 pp. London: Rhinegold Publishing Limited, 1990.

This is a useful handbook, especially geared toward auditioning in the United Kingdom and on the continent, although equally helpful for anyone. It covers auditioning for opera, festivals, competitions, choral work, radio and recording. The author has included addresses and phone numbers of opera companies, agents, festivals and competitions. The larger portion of the text concentrates on operatic repertoire organized by *Fach*. For each entry, Legge who is himself a well-known coach and accompanist, offers commentary on appropriate performance style for auditions. He also includes a brief synopsis of the action taking place when the aria is sung and the range of the aria. Finally, there is a comprehensive list of opera arias, arranged by voice type and then *Fach*.

7.18   Lieberman, Julie Lyonn. *You Are Your Instrument: The Definitive Musician's Guide to Practice and Performance.* 147 pp. New York: Huiksi Music, 1991.

Although this text is geared more at instrumentalists than singers, there is still helpful information to be found. The author discusses performance anxiety, musical injury, tension, and how to overcome them, along with ways to increase learning skills and to create a healthier learning and performing method. She also discusses traveling, pre-performance routines, and other related matters. Also included are guides for healing and relaxation therapies.

7.19   Litherland, Janet, and Sue McAnally. *Broadway Costumes on a Budget: Big-Time Ideas for Amateur Producers.* 146 pp. Colorado Springs, CO: Meriwether Publishing, 1996.

7.20   Lucha-Burns, Carol. *Musical Notes: A Practical Guide to Staffing and Staging Standards of the American Musical Theater.* 581 pp. Westport, Conn.: Greenwood Press, Inc., 1986.

In-depth synopses and significant background information is given for musicals, both the standard and the not-so standard. Numerous lists and indexes including a chronology of productions, "professionals and their specialities," among others.

7.21   Lynch, Richard Chigley. *Musicals! a Complete Selection Guide for Local Productions.* Second edition. 404 pp. Chicago: American Library Association, 1994.

Provides detailed information on approximately 500 musical properties currently available for production. Arranged alphabetically by title, each entry lists composer, lyricist, playwright, date of production, plot summary, original cast and parts played, revival casts, suggested recordings and librettos, and the licensing agent. The author includes an Appendix with the addresses and phone numbers for the licensing agents. Composer/Lyricist/Librettist index. Song title index.

7.22   Miller, Scott. *From Assassins to West Side Story: the Director's Guide to Musical Theatre.* 242 pp. Portsmouth, NH: Heinemann, 1996.

The author, a director, shares his thoughts and perceptions of sixteen musical theater productions as starting places for other directors to begin their own productions of these and other works.   The works included are *Assassins, Cabaret, Carousel, Company, Godspell, Gypsy, How to Succeed in Business Without Really Trying, Into the Woods, Jesus Christ Superstar, Man of La Mancha, Merrily We Roll Along, Les Misérables, My Fair Lady, Pippin, Sweeney Todd,* and *West Side Story.* For each, the author discusses both textual and musical themes, production design, background on the characters, both historical and social context of the action, the intentions of those who created the show, and its social relevance.   Useful reading for anyone involved in a production, not just the director.

7.23   National Association of Schools of Music. *The Education and Training of the Singer-actor.* 81 pp. Reston, Va.: NASM, 1984.

The published report of findings from a survey for NASM in 1981 on the state of musical theater programs in member institutions.   The findings cover curricula, resources, etc., in a cut-and-dry format.   The appendixes include a list of productions between 1980 and 1983 at the participating institutions and the results of a 1983 survey of training/apprentice programs in the United States, which though now many years out of date, provide a core listing of American apprentice programs.

7.24   Novak, Elaine Adams. *Performing in Musicals.* 306 pp. New York: Schirmer Books, 1988.

Essentially a workbook for the beginning student of musical theater.   Chapters include background information on the development of the genre of musical theater, its elements and aspects of production, movement, vocal and acting exercises, audition skills.   A unique feature is the inclusion of scenes for rehearsal and practice, both dialogue and songs.   Bibliography, glossary and index.

7.25   Oliver, Donald. *How to Audition for the Musical Theatre: A Step-by-Step Guide to Effective Preparation.* Revised edition. 141 pp. Lyme, NH: Smith and Kraus, Inc., 1995. (A career development book)

The author, who worked as an audition accompanist in New York for many years, describes this book as a primer for auditioning in musical theater. It is a basic, straight-forward guide for audition preparation and it includes chapters on "What not to sing" and "What to do if you forget the lyrics." Four appendixes provide information on agents, headshots and résumés, names and addresses of bookstores, music stores, etc., and a uniquely-titled section "A partial list of the most overdone uninspired, (and inappropriate) audition songs."

7.26   Pauly, Reinhard G. *Music and the Theater: An Introduction to Opera.* 462 pp. Enlgewood Cliffs, N. J.: Prentice-Hall, Inc., 1970.

Moving chronologically, the text looks at operas that represent different stylistic trends, such as *verismo* and *expressionism*. There are also chapters devoted to the relationship of music and drama, opera production, and opera's position in society.

7.27   *Perspectives: Audition Advice for Singers.* 45 pp. Washington, D. C.: Opera America, 1996.

A collection of twenty-seven essays by teachers, directors, administrators and singers that offer their personal observations about the audition process. Some of the contributors are Plato Karayanis, Michael Ching, Roberta Peters, Evelyn Lear and Thomas Stewart. The essays are short and offer practical advice. Other titles included in the *Perspectives* series include *The Singer/Manager Relationship* (1997) and *Creating and Producing Contemporary Opera in Musical Theater* (1983).

7.28   Porter, Susan L. *With an Air Debonair: Musical Theatre in America, 1785 - 1815.* 631 pp. Washington, D.C.: Smithsonian Institution Press, 1991.

An examination of the development the genre that features a great deal of primary source material. Most pertinent are chapters on the acting traditions, singing styles, and techniques of the day. There are sections devoted to the vocal instrument, training, and ornamentation.   Informative appendixes and bibliography, detailed index. Interested readers should also consult June Ottenberg's *Opera Odyssey: Toward a History of Opera in Nineteenth-century America* (Greenwood Press, 1994) for a study that overlaps a bit chronologically and carries forward up to 1900.

7.29   Priest, Julia. *From Stage-Fright to Seat-Height: An Annotated Bibliography on the Alexander Technique and Music 1907-1992.* 28 pp. North Grosvenordale, Conn.: Julia Priest, P.O. Box 37, 06255, 1993.

Most performers and teachers are familiar with the philosophies of the Alexander technique and its benefits. This bibliography leads the reader to articles, books, and dissertations on the topic, arranged chronologically by format.

7.30   Shea, George E. *Acting in Opera.* 90 pp. New York: Da Capo Press, 1980. (Da Capo Reprint Series)

First published in 1915 by G. Schirmer. The author was, according to the prefatory matter of this reprint, the first American to sing opera in France. Given current day approaches to acting in opera, this monograph offers a wonderful look at the art of acting in opera from a century ago. Shea begins with "How to Walk" and moves on to how and when to gesture, and so on. There are numerous photographs showing examples of the different movements and gestures being discussed.

7.31   Silver, Fred. *Auditioning for the Musical Theatre.* 204 pp. New York: Newmarket Press, 1985.

The author brings more than twenty-five years of experience in the musical theater to this "how-to" book, written for everyone from the high school student to the Broadway professional. Includes a list of recommended audition songs. The foreword, written by Charles Strouse, sets the stage for the book: Auditions last, on the average, fifty-five seconds. The intent of Silver's book is to show singers, actors, and dancers how to "own" that fifty-five seconds.

7.32   Soeby, Lynn M. *Way Off Broadway: A Complete Guide to Producing Musicals with School and Community Groups.* 155 pp. Jefferson, N.C.: McFarland & Company, Inc., 1991.

A practical "how-to" for anyone involved in school or community theater groups. Covers all aspects of producing a musical theater production. Includes a glossary of musical and stage terms.

7.33   Stanislavski, Constantin, and Pavel Rumyantsev. Translated and edited by Elizabeth Reynolds Hapgood. *Stanislavski on Opera*. 374 pp. New York: Theatre Arts Books, 1975.

Rumyantsev was a participant in the Bolshoi's Opera Studio as a student, singer and director, and ultimately playing the title role in *Eugene Onegin*, directed by Stanislavki. This book is, according to its translator, a transcription of Stanislavki's words and work in the opera studio. Here one can read about the great teacher/director's method, his daily work with the students, and his direction of several operas, including *Eugene Onegin, La Bohème, Boris Godunov*, and others.

7.34   Sullivan, Gail, and Dorothy Madison. *Kein' Angst, Baby!* 204 pp. Millburn, N. J.: Clearing Press, 1994.

A book for American singers auditioning in German-speaking countries, written by American singers. It includes suggestions for how to plan auditions and how to set a budget. It also includes sample letters of inquiry and resumes. Most importantly, it includes a repertoire listing organized by Fach and a directory of opera houses in Austria, Germany, and Switzerland.

7.35   Summers, W. Franklin. *Operas in One Act: A Production Guide*. 383 pp. Lanham, MD: The Scrarecrow Press, 1997.

Prof. Franklin teaches voice and opera history at the University of Miami School of Music and is in charge of its opera program. In his preface, he states that the purpose of this book is to "provide assistance to anyone concerned with the selection of operas in one-act for production or simply to provide general information pertaining to these works" (p. vii). It lists over 275 operas, with each entry including some or all of the following information: composer and dates, title, libretto, duration, cast, chorus, dance, instrumentation, piano accompaniment, style, setting, scenes, synopsis, production notes, premiere, materials. Divided into two parts: operas written in English and operas with English translations. Indexes for composers, titles, durations, and publishers and sources.

7.36   Tarr Krüger, Irmtraud. *Performance Power: Transforming Stress into Creative Energy*. Translated by Dr. Edward H. Tarr. 252 pp. Tempe, Ariz.: Summit Books, 1995.

Offers the reader practical advice and useful exercises to overcome performance anxiety. The author is both an active concert organist and psychotherapist and has written other publications dealing with stress management. This particular volume examines the variety of problems that are related to performance anxiety and offers a holistic approach for dealing with it.

7.37   Van Witsen, Leo. *Costuming for Opera: Who Wears What and Why*. 232 pp. Bloomington, Ind.: Indiana University Press, 1981. Volume II. 354 pp. Metuchen, N. J.: The Scarecrow Press, Inc., 1994.

This noted costume designer examines some thirty operas and his costuming ideas and suggestions for them. Countless drawings and photographs provide ample examples. The glossary in the first volume is reproduced in the second, without illustrations. Bibliographies in both.

7.38   Wallace, Mary Elaine, and Robert Wallace. *Opera Scenes for Class and Stage*. 260 pp. Carbondale, IL: Southern Illinois University Press, 1979.

There are two primary sections: the first "Table of Voice Categories" in which can be found suggested scenes for virtually any combination and number of voice types. Indications for chorus, speaking parts and so on are included. The second section, arranged alphabetically by title, provides the composer's name and dates, the duration, available piano-vocal scores and page numbers, and a brief synopsis. Bibliography. Indexes of operas, composers, arias and ensembles, and editions of piano-vocal scores. A later volume by the same authors, *More Opera Scenes for Class and Stage: From One Hundred Selected Operas*, emphasizes contemporary opera.

7.39   Warren, Raymond. *Opera Workshop: Studies in Understanding and Interpretation*. 279 pp. Aldershot, England: Scolar Press, 1995.

An examination of the way in which the various components of an opera combine to create the whole. There is discussion of how the orchestra "supports the singer" and how it "enlarges the stage."

8

Travel and Education

8.1   Adams, Richard. *A Book of British Music Festivals.*   224 pp.
London: Robert Rouce; Riverdale Md.: Riverdale, 1986.

Lists pertinent information for approximately 200 festivals in Great Britain.
Includes a map, calendar, and festival addresses.

8.2   Balázs, István. *Musical Guide to Hungary.* 160 pp.   Budapest:
Corvina, 1992.

Provides necessary travel information such as maps, addresses, phone numbers,
and ticket information as well as an overview of musical life in Hungary.

8.3   Bernstein, Ken. *Music Lovers' Europe: A Guidebook and Companion.*
202 pp. New York: Scribner's, 1983.

Arranged alphabetically by country and offers a wide variety of information about
travelling abroad.

8.4   Brody, Elaine and Claire Brook. *The Music Guide to Great Britain.*
240 pp. New York: Dodd, Mead & Company, 1975.

Although some information is outdated at this point in time, this guide and its partner volumes, provides useful information for anyone preparing to travel to any number of locales. A sampling of the types of information includes guides and services, opera houses and concert halls, libraries and museums, musical monuments, schools, organizations, instrument sales and repair, retail music shops and so forth. Companion volumes are *The Music Guide to Austria and Germany* (1975); *The Music Guide to Belgium, Luxembourg, Holland and Switzerland* (1977) and *The Music Guide to Italy* (1978).

8.5   Burton, Gary. *A Musician's Guide to the Road.* 156 pp. New York: Watson-Guptill Publications, 1981.

Necessary information for travelling musicians of all kinds.

8.6   Campbell, James. R. *Festival Fever: The Ultimate Guide to Musical Celebrations in the Northeast.* 858 pp. Glen Ridge, N. J.: FestPress, 1995.

A guide to events in Connecticut, Maine, Massachusetts, New Hampshire, New York, and Rhode Island.

8.7   Clynes, Tom. *Musical Festivals from Bach to Blues: A Traveller's Guide.* 582 pp. Detroit, MI: Visible Ink Press, 1996.

8.8   Couch, John Philip. *The Opera Lover's Guide to Europe.* 256 pp. New York: Limelight Editions, 1991.

Although the larger European cities and houses are included, the focus is more on the smaller cities.

8.9   Cowden, Robert H. *Opera Companies of the World: Selected Profiles.* 336 pp. New York: Greenwood Press, 1992.

Background information on over 180 major opera companies. Entries include information on the city and the company itself, both historical and current, along with phone and fax numbers, addresses, etc. Many entries include short bibliographies.

8.10   Geddes, Murray, and Alec Tebbutt. *European Summer Music Festivals*. 291 pp. Toronto: Concert Connection, 1980.

Lists more than 200 festivals in twenty-six countries. Includes all pertinent information and also provides maps of the countries and translation charts of important, concert-related words.

8.11   Gottesman, Roberta, editor. *The Music Lover's Guide to Europe: A Compendium of Festivals, Concerts, and Opera*. 434 pp. New York: John Wiley & Sons, Inc., 1992.

A useful tool for planning European holidays around musical experiences. Arranged alphabetically by country, although Scandinavian countries are grouped together, as are those in Eastern Europe. Portugal and Spain are also grouped together. Each chapter includes a map of the country, a calendar, and a city-by-city listing of events and pertinent related information, such as box office addresses, phone and fax numbers.

8.12   *Guide to Competitions*. 11th ed., expanded and rev. 132 pp. New York: Concert Artists Guild, 1997.

Up-to-date information on vocal competitions all over the world, along with listings for instrumentalists and conductors.

8.13   Lebrecht, Norman. *Music in London: A History and Handbook*. 183 pp. London: Aurum Press Limited, 1992. Published originally in Frence by B. Coutaz (Bouches-du-Rhône, 1991).

Includes a chronology of music since the days of Roman occupation, historical essays, and information on concerts and places to visit. Readers should also consult Edward Lee's *Musical London* (London: Omnibus Press, 1995).

8.14   Leon, Ruth. *Applause: New York's Guide to the Performing Arts*. 506 pp. New York: Applause Books, 1991.

A place to find everything from ticket costs to subway directions along with information on concerts, opera, jazz, theater, festivals, and so on. Other useful information includes wheelchair accessibility, hearing devices and a section on activities for children.

8.15   Plantamura, Carol. *The Opera Lover's Guide to Europe.* 338 pp. Secaucus, N. J.: Citadel/Carol Publishing Group, 1996.

An operatic guidebook to forty-seven European locations, mostly Italian. Includes everything from maps and drawings of opera houses and other sites of interest to travel tips (e.g., the sign for a bus stop in Italy is a *fermata* and is clearly marked as such) and background information on relevant composers and operas. Schedules for opera houses and restaurant tips are also included. There is a glossary and an index.

8.16   Rabin, Carol Price. *Music Festivals in America: Classical, Opera, Jazz, Pops, Country, Old-Time Fiddlers, Folk, Bluegrass, Cajun.* 4th edition. 271 pp. Great Barrington, Mass.: Berkshire Traveller Press, 1990.

First published in 1979 under the title *A Guide to Music Festivals in America.* Lists information 160 events. Arranged by genre, rock music being the only exclusion.

8.17   Rabin, Carol Price. *Music Festivals in Europe and Britain: Including Israel, Russia, Turkey and Japan.* Revised and enlarged. 191 pp. Stockbridge, Mass.: Berkshire Traveller Press, 1984.

Previously published in 1980. Lists well over 100 festivals in twenty-seven countries, including information on history and locations, accomodations and tickets, etc.

8.18   Rossi, Nick. *Opera in Italy Today: A Guide.* 420 pp. Portland, Ore,: Amadeus Press, 1995.

Offers information on opera houses large and small as well as festivals. Seasons, ticket information and addresses.

8.19   Sonel, Claudette. *Mind Your Musical Manners -- On and Off Stage. A Handbook of Stage Etiquette.* 3rd edition. 80 pp. Milwaukee: E. B. Marks Co., 1995.

Includes a listing of competitions held both in the U.S. and abroad.

8.20   Stockdale, F. M., and M. R. Dreyer. *The International Opera Guide.* 342 pp. North Pomfret, Vt.: Trafalgar Square, 1990.

Divided in two sections, the first being a guide to 97 major opera houses and companies, offering information on everything from history and repertoire to length of season, street maps, and credit cards accepted. The second section lists composers and their operas. There is also a short list of opera festivals which is arranged by country.

8.21   Turnbull, Robert. *The Opera Gazetteer.* 240 pp. London: Trefoil Publications, Ltd., 1988.

Listing 114 opera houses throughout the world, this book provides background information on the houses and resident companies along with the companies' directors, seasons, seating capacity, box office hours of operation, phone numbers and addresses, prices and discounts, and so forth. Many photographs. A two-page, sixteen-word glossary and an index conclude the book.

8.22   Zeitz, Karyl Lynn. *Opera Companies and Houses of the United States.* 335 pp. Jefferson, N. C.: McFarland & Company, Inc., 1995.

Arranged alphabetically by state. The following information is given for each: a brief background essay on both the company and the facility, names of general and artistic directors, world and American premieres, repertoire, and practical information such as addresses, phone numbers and ticket information. Numerous photographs.

Education and Music Business

8.23   Davidson, John, and Cort Casady. *The Singing Entertainer: A Contemporary Study of the Art and Business of Being a Professional.* Newly rev. ed. 240 pp. Sherman Oaks, Calif.: Alred, 1982.

Includes discussions on budget and saving money, the music business, maintaining vocal health. The book also stresses the importance of continuing to expand one's talents.

8.24   Everett, Carole. *The Performing Arts Major's College Guide.* 2nd ed. 301 pp. New York: Macmillan, 1994.

Written by the director of admissions for The Juilliard School, this guide offers practical advice for selecting a school and preparing for auditions. There are listings for which schools are better for voice or different instruments and the author includes background information on a long list of schools.

8.25   Giacobello, John. *Choosing a Career in Music.* 64 pp. New York: Rosen Publishing Group, 1997. (The World of Work)

8.26   Highstein, Ellen. *Making Music in Look Glass Land: A Guide to Survival and Business Skills for the Classical Musician.* 2nd ed. 260 pp. New York: Concert Artists Guild, 1993.

Offers sound, practical advice to young performers preparing to embark on their professional careers. Includes a chapter on competitions.

8.27   Hoover, Deborah A. *Supporting Yourself as an Artist.* 255 pp. New York: Oxford University Press, 1989.

The author provides all sorts of "nuts and bolts" information for any artist hoping to make a living in his or her chosen field. Includes information on business, legal and financial aspects, along with appendices for resumé writing and addresses of foundations, arts councils, etc.

8.28   Papolos, Janice. *The Performing Artist's Handbook.* 219 pp. Cincinnati, Oh.: Writer's Digest Books, 1984.

A useful guide to the business of being a performer: marketing, networking, legal aspects, and so forth. The author writes from her own personal experiences and shares "dos and don'ts" on everything from picking the best headshot to tax deductions and mailing lists.

8.29   *Peterson's Professional Degree Programs in the Visual and Performing Arts 1997.* 587 pp. Princeton, N. J.: Peterson's Guides, 1997.

Provides information on some 400 programs in the United States and Canada.

8.30   Pickard, Wayland. *Complete Singer's Guide to Becoming a Working Professional* 195 pp. Studio City, Calif.: Pickard Publishing, 1992.

A "how-to" geared for pop singers that covers topics such as stage presence, microphone techniques, structuring a set, auditioning, touring, and promotion, among many others. Also includes "Communicating with the Band in Their Vocabulary," which is a vocabulary listing of, for the most part, standard musical terms. The reader will also find here definitions for more colorful terms such as "the ink is good"(play the chart as written) and "lotsa footballs" (a string of whole notes).

8.31   Summers-Dossena, Ann. *Getting It All Together: A Handbook for Performing Artists in Classical Music and Ballet.* 179 pp. Metuchen, N. J. and London: The Scarecrow Press, Inc., 1985.

The author is an artist's manager and offers young, beginning performers information the will "guide artists in identifying and setting the course in developing their own careers; to encourage those interested in management to accept apprenticeships or internships; and to emphasize the need for educational institutes to instill a sense of awareness and professionalism in their students" (p. xvi).

8.32   Towse, Ruth. *Singers in the Marketplace: The Economics of the Singing Profession.* 252 pp. Oxford: Clarendon Press, 1993.

A report on an economic study of the singing profession in Britain between 1988 and 1990, written by a singer who is also an economist. Chapter headings include "The Provision for Training Classical Singers in Britain," "The Cost of Training Singers," "Employment in the Market for Singers," "Factors Affecting the Demand for Singers," and in the third part of the study, "The Earnings of Singers" and "The Rate of Return to Training as a Singer." There are three appendixes, including "The Training and Employment of Singers in Germany." Bibliography, index.

9

Internet and Electronic Resources

Print Guides to Electronic Resources

9.1   Ehn, Hope. *On-Line Resources for Classical and Academic Musicians: A Guide through the Wilds of the Internet: Newsgroups, Mailing Lists, and Other Resources for Early Music, Classical Music, Musicology, Music Theory and Ethnomusicology, with a Guide to Basic List-Serve Commands for Subscribing to Mailing Lists and to Getting Files by E-Mail.* 40 pp. Newton Centre, Mass.: The Author, 1994.

A "how-to" guide for virtually any on-line resource dealing with music.

9.2   Gurley, Ted. *Plug In: The Guide to Music on the Net.* 320 pp. + compact disc. Upper Saddle River, N. J.: Prentice-Hall, 1996.

Information and how to find it for any type of music or musician on the Internet.

9.3   Hill, Brad. *The Virtual Musician: A Complete Guide to Online Resources and Services.* 257 pp. + compact disc. New York: Schirmer Books, 1996.

A primer and guidebook to the many resources, services and sites available to musicians on the Internet. A similar book by Gary Hustwit is entitled *The Musician's Guide to the Internet* (Hal Leonard, 1996).

9.4   Waters, William J. *Music and the Personal Computer: An Annotated Bibliography.* 175 pp. New York: Greenwood Press, 1989. (Music reference collection, 22)

Lists over 1200 entries that lead the reader to information about computers and music.

Online Resources

9.5   *The Aria Database.* [http://www.aria-database.com]

Searchable by name, opera, language or voice type. Includes translations, libretto and MIDI files. Complete listings for Mozart, Verdi and others. Discography for many selections. Current statistical information for the database lists 609 arias, seventy-six operas. twenty-six composers, 137 translations and fifty-four MIDI files.

9.6   *Classics World Performers.* [http://classicalmus.com/bmgclassics/perf-index/artist-voice.html]

Biographies and discographies of singers, including Elly Ameling, Marian Anderson, Montserrat Caballé, Enrico Caruso, Placido Domingo, Christa Ludwig, Jan Peerce, and many others.

9.7   *College Music Society.* [http://www.music.org]

The College Music Society (CMS) is a consortium of music schools and departments as well as individual scholars and musicians. The goal of the organization, as stated on the home page is to be "united by a dedication to the science of learning and the art of teaching" and to be "engaged in a dialogue that will shape music teaching in the years ahead." This site offers information on membership, regional chapters, activities and governance. It also offers addresses of music schools, departments, and conservatories, links to music organizations, music information sources, and many others. Readers should take note of the British site known as the *Golden Pages: University Music Departments' and Faculties' Home Pages,* maintained by Geoffrey Chew:
[http://www.sun.rhbnc.ac.uk/Music/Links/musdepts.html]

9.8   *Foreign Language Dictionaries Online.*
          [http://copper.ucs.indiana.edu/~lneff/fordict.html]

Provides access to a number of dictionaries, helpful for translations.

9.9   *Gaylord Music Library Necrology File.*   (Washington University).
          [http://library.wustl.edu/~music/necro/]

Begun in 1991, this is a good place to locate death dates of composers and
performers. Maintained by Nathan Eakin. Readers should also consult the Music
Library Association's Obituary Index, located at the URL [http://www-
sul.stanford.edu/depts/music/mla/necrology/welcome.html] which provides not
only the death dates of the individual, but also cites journal and dictionaries
where further biographical information may be found.

9.10   *Gilbert and Sullivan Collection.* (Pierpont Morgan Library, New York)
          [http://www.nyu.edu/pages/curator/gs/]

Information on the most significant collection of G & S materials. See also the
Gilbert and Sullivan Archive at [http://diamond.idgsu.edu/gas/GaS.html].

9.11   *IPA Association Webpage.*
          [http://www.arts.gla.ac.uk/IPA/ipachart.html]

Full IPA chart, fonts, sounds, and examnations.

9.12   *Italian Music Homepage.* [http://ic1382.cilea.it/music/entrance.htm]

Available in both English and Italian. Lists access to Italian music libraries,
services and universities, music schools, opera houses, musical events, Italian
music publishers, etc. Compiled by Massimo Gentili-Tedeschi.

9.13   *Lieder and Songs: Texts.* [http://www.recmusic.org/lieder/]

Access to texts that are in public domain. Maintained by Emily Ezust.

9.14   *Lully Web Project.*
        [http://www.library.unt.edu:80/projects/lully/lullyhom.html]

A place to locate information about Lully's stage works, based at the University
of North Texas. UNT's Music Library owns many first and second editions of
these works. Maintained by Dorothy Keyser.

9.15   *Musicals.Net.* [http://musicals.net]

Information on a long list of musicals, access to *Playbill*, and other
miscellaneous information.

9.16   *Opera America.* [http://www.operaam.org/]

The homepage for the association by the same name which offers support and
resources to the opera community, including many valuable publications,
programs and membership information.

9.17   *Opera Libretti and Other Vocal Texts.*
        [http://copper.ucs.indiana.edu/~lneff/libretti.html]

Includes libretti for opera and oratorio in the original language that are in public
domain. Maintained by Lyle Neff.

9.18   *Opera Schedule Server.* [http://www.fsz.bme.hu.opera/main.html]

Information on schedules, individual companies, and links to other opera-related
sources. Some of the companies included are Pacific Opera Victoria, Seattle
Opera, Atlanta Opera, The Hunstville Opera Theater, and West Bay Opera and
others.

9.19   *Operabase.* [http://www.operabase.com]

Available in English, Italian, French, German and Spanish. The database offers
information on opera houses, festivals, performances and artists. Includes
information on television and radio broadcast schedules. Compiled by Mike
Gibb. See also *OperaGlass* at [http://rick.stanford.edu/opera/main.html] and
OperaWeb at [http://www.opera.it/English/OperaWeb.html] for similar
information.

9.20   *RCA Victor Red Seal Opera Treasury.*
        [http://classicalmus.com/bmgclassics/opera/index.html

Access to information on opera and opera recordings. Includes some synopses
and information for ordering recordings.

9.21   *Russian Music.* [http://mars.uthscsa.edu/Russia/Music]

Includes information on Russian opera singers.

9.22   *Texaco-Metropolitan Opera.*
        [http://www.texaco.com/met/methome.htm]

Information on the Texaco-sponsored radio broadcasts, listing of radio stations
that carry the broadcasts, related background information, and information on the
current season.

9.23   *Virtual Opera House.* [http://196.27.35.6/users/dlever]

General information about opera, including an online glossary of operatic terms.

9.24   URLs for opera companies. Listed here are addresses for a selection of
        opera companies throughout the United States and elsewhere. Generally
        speaking, the sites include information on the season, tickets,
        background information on the company, and links to other
        organizations and resources.

Cleveland Opera. [http://www.clevopera.com]
The Dallas Opera. [http://www.dallasopera.org]
English National Opera.
        [http://www.gold.ac.uk/~mut01sp/opera/ENO/eno.html]
Finnish National Opera. [http://www.kolumbus.fi/opera/english.htm]
La Scala. [http://lascala.milano.it/]
Los Angeles Music Center Opera (L. A. Opera). [http://www.laopera.org]
Metropolitan Opera [http://www.metopera/org]
New York City Opera. [http://www.nycopera.com]
Opera Carolina. [http://www.operacarolina.com]
Opera Colorado. [http://www.aescon.com/music/opcol/index.shtml]

Opera Delaware. [http://www.operadel.org]
Opera Pacific. [http://www.ocartsnet.org/opera_pacific]
Pittsburgh Opera. [http://www.contrib.andrew.cmu.edu/usr/dma4/popera.html]
Royal Opera House. Covent Garden. http://195.26.96.12/house/
Royal Swedish Opera House. [http://www.dataphone.se/~gberkson/operan]
San Diego Opera. [http://www.sdopera.com]
San Francisco Opera. [http://www.sfopera.com]
Santa Fe Opera. [http://www.santafeopera.org]
Sydney Opera House. [http://www.sydneyoperahouse.nsw.gov.au]
Vienna State Opera. [http://austria-info.at/kultur/ws-wv/index.html]
The Washington Opera. [http://www.dc-opera.org]

9.25   *OPERA-L.* (Mailing list)

An open forum for discussion on opera and related issues.   Maintained at the
City University of New York. To subscribe, send the message "sub OPERA-L
your name" to listserv@cunyvm.cuny.edu.   To post a message to the group,
send it to opera-l@cunyvm.cuny.edu

9.26   *rec.music.opera.* (Newsgroup)

A forum for discussion on all aspects of opera.   This is a Usenet newsgroup
located on the Internet.

9.27   *rec.arts.theatre.musicals.* (Newsgroup)

Open forum of discussion on musical theater.

Databases

9.28   *Arts & Humanities Search.* 1 datafile.   Philadelphia, Pa.: Institute for
        Scientific Information.

Access to citations for 1,100 arts and humanities journals from all over the
world. Includes reviews of books, scores, music, and theatrical performances.
Begun in 1980, this is a partner to the printed version, *Arts & Humanities
Citaion Index,* and is also available through OCLC's *FirstSearch* under the title
A&H Search.

9.29   *Billboard/Phonolog Music Reference Library on CD-ROM.* 1 CD-ROM. New York: BPI Communications, 1992- . Updated quarterly.

Over 100,000 recorded songs, searchable by title, label, artist or group, composer, conductor, orchestra, or instrument.

9.30   *Dissertation Abstracts Online: A FirstSearch Database.* Ann Arbor, Mich.: Dissertation Publishing, 1986- .

Provides access to almost every American dissertation accepted by accredited institutions since 1861. Includes selected master's theses beginning in 1962. Citations for Canadian dissertations, as well as from institutions from abroad. Coincides with *Dissertation Abstracts International* and *Masters Abstracts*, both published by University Microfilms International.

9.31   *International Index to Music Periodicals.* 1 CD-ROM. Alexandria, Va.: Chadwyck-Healey, 1996- .

Extensive database of articles published in over 400 scholarly music journals. Searchable by author, title, publication, country, date, language, article type, subject heading, and so on. There is also a web version.

9.32   *The Music Catalog.* 1 CD-ROM. Washington, D. C.: Library of Congress, 1994- .

Contains all music-related records from the Library of Congress database; records describing the Albert Schatz Collection of Opera Librettos (11,380 records) and Library of Congress PreMARC records for opera librettos, scores and sound recordings (30,000 records).

9.33   *MUZE: The Ultimate Mind for Music.* 1 CD-ROM. New York: Muze, Inc., 1994- .

Information on 100,000 CDs, cassettes, and videos. Includes information on performers, release dates, durations, as well as biographical information on composers, conductors, and soloists.

10

Periodicals

10.1   *American Music Teacher.*

Published under the title *Music Teachers National Association Bulletin,* 1939-1950. Publication under the current title began in 1951, it has been issued bimonthly since 1961. The organization's membership consists primarily of private or studio teachers. Regular features include reports from various officers, convention news, information about competitions and scholarships, reviews of books and music, and letters to the editor. Other regular columns include "You and Your Finances" and "Studio Tips," among others. There are several articles in each issue that pertain either to teaching or to music and the overall goal of the organization and this journal is to promote professionalism among its members.

10.2   *American Record Guide.*

First published in 1935 as *The American Music Lover.* Before changing to its present title in October 1944, there was one issue published in September, the *Listener's Record Guide.* It has been issued six times annually since 1982. Its purpose is to offer information and reviews on recordings for the "serious" music lover. Here the reader will find reviews of operas and musical theater amongst approximately one hundred reviews included in each issue. Reviews include background on the piece, an assessment of the performance along with comparisons to other performances, technical quality, available formats, contents and pricing information.

10.3   *Association for Recorded Sound Collections Journal.*

This journal, primarily geared towards discographers, was begun in 1967. It is published three times per year. This is a good place to look for discographies for artists and composers, along with series such as "World's Greatest Operas."

10.4   *Cambridge Opera Journal.*

Published three times per year. Interdisciplinary in its scope, emphasis leans towards early opera and twentieth-century opera.

10.5   *Early Music.*

A journal for anyone interested in early music and its performance. A good source for information on performance practice, individual composers, interpretation, and so forth, the journal's predominating tone is that of practicality for the performer. There are reviews of books, printed music, and recordings in each issue. Of special interest is the "Register of Early Music," which was an international directory of performers and ensembles that was discontinued in 1978.

10.6   *Fanfare; The Magazine for Serious Record Collectors.*

Published six times per year. Includes interviews, discographies, and many, many reviews of recordings.

10.7   *The Gramophone.*

An outstanding resource for reviews of sound and video recordings, along with timely articles on the world of classical music. The reviews are divided into groupings so readers can go directly to the sections on opera and choral and on song. Copious advertisements and the monthly Editor's "top ten" allow the reader every opportunity to stay on the cutting edge.

10.8   *The Journal of Singing.*

The official journal of the National Association of Teachers of Singing (NATS) was first published as *The NATS Bulletin* from 1944 to 1984 and then as *The NATS Journal* from 1985 until 199--.   Five issues per year are published bimonthly, with no issue for July/August.   The purpose of the journal has always been to promote sound vocal education.   There are always pedagogical articles, columns on vocal science and new music; book, music, and recordings reviews; and information about the organization. A related title, which has ceased publication is *Journal of Research in Singing and Applied Vocal Pedagogy.*

10.9   *Journal of Voice: Official Journal of the Voice Foundation.*

A quarterly medical journal that concentrates on clinical vocal science and arts medicine. *Medical Problems of Performing Artists* is another journal that concentrates on the care and treatment of medical disabilities related to the arts.

10.10   *Music and Musicians.*

The first issue of this monthly journal appeared in 1952 and since that time it has dealt with the English classical music scene.   The issue numbers correspond to the concert season so the September issue is always the first of the volume. Topics covered in the articles include current musical events, popular classical musicians, opera productions, and so on.

10.11   *The Music Review.*

This quarterly journal is directed primarily towards the music theorist and musicologist; however, readers will find the occasional analysis of an opera that will prove beneficial to research.

10.12   *Musical America.*

Reports on the concert scene in the U. S. and includes regular columns on highlights, education, television, new music, book reviews and personalities. Each issue features a "Musician of the Month," complete with cover photograph and an interview.   There is also information on competitions, awards and appointments as well as "Debuts and Reappearances."   Begun in 1898, the journal was incorporated into *High Fidelity* from 1965 to 1988, and then once again published on its own afterwards.

10.13   *Musical Times.*

This British monthly journal has been in existence since 1844 and was first published by Novello and Company. It was originally titled *The Musical Times and Singing Class Circular*, dropping the second half of the title in 1904. It began as a means to get music to the working class. As the music periodical with the longest consecutive publishing history, it has undergone many changes. Today it is a place to locate interesting articles on all aspects of music, reviews of books, music, and recordings, reviews of concerts in London and elsewhere, announcements of all sorts, including audition notices for choral singers, and the "London Musical Diary" which lists coming events.

10.14   *19th Century Music.*

A scholarly journal published three times yearly. Given the musical period covered, it is no surprise to be led to this journal for articles on opera. Readers will also find information on music festivals, editions, among other things in "Comment and Chronicle," a regular feature of the journal.

10.15   *New York Opera Newsletter.*

Subtitled "The Classical Singer's Magazine" this monthly publication packs a great deal of information into each issue; most importantly, auditions, competitions, ads for teachers and coaches, workshops and seminars, and so forth. There are articles about young singers who are "making it," along with health or business-related articles. All in all, quite useful.

10.16   *NOTES, The Quarterly Journal of the Music Library Association.*

In publication since 1937 under variations of the same name, this is the longest-running journal pertaining to music librarianship. Issues are always full of book and score reviews, lists of books and scores received, reviews of new periodicals (once annually), a necrology (once annually), articles, and until recently, an index to record reviews. Although it is a "library" journal, its readership extends far beyond music librarians. Any musician, teacher or student will find value in the book reviews and the lists of new scores, books and periodicals.

10.17   *Opera.*

Published monthly with an annual festival issue. Its first editor was the Earl of Harewood. It chronicles current operatic events on an international level and includes interesting articles on operas, performers, composers, and so on. Within each issue is a "Coming Events" section, easily located due to its being on differently-colored paper. This section lists future events, both in England and abroad. The Festival issue covers summer events, including Glyndebourne.

10.18   *Opera Australia.*

Monthly periodical that covers opera and musical theater for Australasian locales. Includes reviews of productions, books recordings, and videos.

10.19   *Opera Canada.*

Monthly journal devoted to opera, both in Canada and elsewhere. In publication since 1960. Another Canadian publication, *Performing Arts in Canada*, focuses more broadly on theater, dance, music and film.

10.20   *Opera Journal.*

A scholarly journal on operatic subjects published by the National Opera Association (NOA). Also includes reviews of books and scores and information about NOA.

10.21   *Opera News.*

Seventeen issues per year, being published biweekly, December through April, and monthy, May through November. Here readers will find current news on established opera stars as well as rising ones; castlists, synopses, and photographs for both the Saturday radio broadcasts and television broadcasts from the Met; reviews of books, videos, and recordings; reviews of performances from all over the U. S. and abroad, schedules of upcoming performances throughout

America, and so forth. Subscribers to *Opera News* may also access the web version of the journal at <http://www.operanews.com/index.htm].

10.22   *Opera Quarterly.*

Intended for scholars, performers, and lovers of opera.   Several articles are included in each issue, as are reviews of books and recordings. There is also an "Opera Quiz" included.

10.23   *Ovation: America's Classical Music Monthly.*

Geared towards a general readership, the journal boasts regional editions and features news and articles on classical music performers.

10.24   *The Record Collector: A Magazine for Collectors of Recorded Vocal Art.*

Focuses on biographies, discographies, and anything else that relates to singers and their recordings.

Author Index

Adam, Nicky, 1.1
Adams, K. Gary, 2.55
Adams, Richard, 8.1
Adler, Kurt, 4.27
Agricola, Johann Friedrich, 6.53
Alderson, Richard, 6.1
Allen, Jeffrey Lee, 6.67
Almquist, Sharon G., 5.22
Alper, Steven M., 7.1
Alton, Jeannine, 3.41
Ammer, Christine, 0.22
Anderson, James, 1.2
Antokoletz, Elliott, 2.55
Appelman, Dudley Ralph, 6.2
Appleby, David P., 2.54
Ardoin, John, 6.3
Arias, Enrique Alberto, 2.54
Austin, David L., 2.54
Avrashov, Regina, 3.59

Bagnoli, Giorgio, 1.3
Bailey, Walter B., 2.54
Baird, Julianne C., 6.53
Baker, David N., 6.68
Balay, Robert, 0.4
Balázs, István, 8.2

Balk, H. Wesley, 7.2
Banfield, Stephen, 2.41
Barber, Josephine, 1.42
Barkelow, Patricia, 2.1
Basart, Ann P., 0.53
Bashford, Christina, 0.12, 1.22
Baumann, Thomas, 3.1
Bayne, Pauline Shaw, 2.1
Beckett, Lucy, 3.1
Beeman, William O., 7.12
Benford, Harry, 1.4
Benser, Caroline Cepin, 2.54
Bernac, Pierre, 4.1
Bernstein, Ken, 8.3
Berry, Corre, 2.2, 2.36
Bird, George, 3.23
Birkin, Kenneth, 3.1
Block, Geoffrey Holden, 1.26, 2.54
Bloom, Ken, 1.27, 1.28
Blyth, Alan, 5.1, 5.2, 5.23
Boldrey, Richard, 2.31, 2.32
Borchgrevink, Hans M., 6.5
Bordman, Gerald, 1.29
Borroff, Edith, 2.33
Bortin, Virginia, 2.54
Bowles, Garrett H., 2.54

Title Index

Subject Index

About the Compiler

RUTHANN BOLES McTYRE is an Assistant Professor and Head Librarian at the Crouch Music and Fine Arts Library at Baylor University. She received her M.L.I.S. degree from the University of North Texas and a graduate degree in vocal performance from the Southern Methodist University. She is an active member of the Music Library Association.

ISBN 0-313-30266-9

90000>

EAN

9 780313 302664

HARDCOVER BAR CODE